Acclaim for *Action in Waiting*

Rodney Clapp, author, *A Peculiar People*
Pulse-quickening…In plain but vibrant language,
Blumhardt reminds us that personal peace is merely the
wrapping paper of a greater, even more magnificent gift:
confidence in the coming of God's kingdom.

Clark Pinnock, author, *The Flame of Love*
Blumhardt is filled with hope about the power of God
to transform the world in concrete ways…His is a holy
optimism grounded not in human prowess but in the
triumphant grace of God.

Donald G. Bloesch, author, *Wellsprings of Renewal*
The modern church needs to hear this social prophet.
Here is a summons to act in confidence and courage in
the firm expectation that God's kingdom is at hand.

Robert Webber, author, *People of the Truth*
Proclaims a message that is indispensable for post-
modern Christianity: Jesus is victor over all the powers
and we, the people of God, are called to live out the
politics radically.

Vernard Eller, author, *Christian Anarchy*
Blumhardt believes that God can make "all" things
new. He challenges us to participate in this newness
and devote ourselves to it.

Dale W. Brown, author, *Biblical Pacifism*
Blumhardt represents a wonderful union of eschatology
and ethics with his focus on the coming and breaking in
of the kingdom of righteousness, justice, love, and peace.

John Miller, *Mennonite Quarterly Review*
One feels these words were shaped for the hour in which we are all living. We have scholars and theologians, but we are almost totally lacking in authentic witnesses to the coming of God's kingdom.

William Dyrness, author, *Let the Earth Rejoice*
Reading Christoph Blumhardt is like drinking from a pure, cold, mountain stream. It is just the tonic we frantic post-moderns need…I always knew what an impact Blumhardt had made on Karl Barth, but after reading him I know why.

Eugene H. Peterson, author, *Subversive Spirituality*
On a landscape increasingly (and depressingly) eroded by world-accommodating strategies and programs, Blumhardt stands as a stark and commanding figure on the horizon. His life and writings are adrenalin for faltering and compromised followers of Jesus.

Stanley Hauerwas, co-author, *Resident Aliens*
That Barth saw Blumhardt's significance is surely not accidental. Who else besides Barth is so unrelenting in their attack on religion? Who else reminds us that Christianity is about the worship and service of a strange God indeed? Who else uses the language of faith so straightforwardly and without apology? The fact that Plough has now made Blumhardt's work available is itself, as Barth would have put it, "a hastening that waits."

Action in
Waiting

Action in Waiting

Christoph Blumhardt

Foreword by Rodney Clapp
Afterword by Karl Barth

The Plough Publishing House

© 1998 by The Plough Publishing House
of The Bruderhof Foundation

Farmington PA 15437 USA
Robertsbridge East Sussex TN32 5DR UK

Cover photograph: Christoph Burki / Tony Stone Images

First Printing: 1998
Second Printing: 1998

A catalog record for this book is available
from the British Library.

Library of Congress Cataloging-in-Publication Data

Blumhardt, Christoph, 1842–1919
    [Selections. English. 1998]
    Action in waiting / Christoph Blumhardt.
            p.   cm.
    ISBN 0-87486-954-4 (pbk.)
    1. Christian life--Lutheran authors.   I. Title.
BX8080.B614A25   1998
230'. 044--dc21   98-15381
                                                          CIP

Printed in the USA

Contents

Foreword

A prominent pastor of our day concludes one of his books with these words:

> I'm enjoying God these days. He answers my prayers. He empowers me. He gives me insights from his Word. He guides my life. He gives me loving relationships. He has wonderful things in store for me.

"I," "my," "me," "me," "me." Is this what the kingdom of God come in Christ is about? God catering to and pampering individual Christians? Is God's rule centered on "me" and "mine"? And on an inner life of insights and guidance set off from the vicissitudes of the world? If so, then I can only sound alarm and paraphrase the apostle Paul – then we Christians are "of all people most to be pitied" (1 Cor. 15:19).

I write these words at the end of a week in which two Arkansas schoolchildren, ages eleven and thirteen, have gunned down classmates and a teacher with high-powered rifles. Darkness bears down on us in many other ways: deepening poverty in American cities and rural areas, ongoing and desperate racial tensions, climbing teenage suicide rates, and dozens of other profound human problems. Suffering and crisis are not confined to the United States, of course. The Middle East daily

stays just a gesture or two away from lethal violence.
The former Slovakian republics stagger barely, if at all,
toward some kind of healing after a decade of barbari-
ties. South Africa and other African nations attempt
bold experiments in reconciliation and democracy, while
all witnessing, knowing how precarious such experiments are, hold their breath. Meanwhile the entire globe
wants most to follow North America in its wanton
accumulation, its wasteful fashions, and the grossest
elements of its popular culture.

Abortion and infanticide. Ecological destruction.
Hatred and misunderstanding between the sexes.
Scientific hubris. The legalization of euthanasia, as respect for the elderly dwindles. A global economy built
and sustained on such inanities as "he who dies with
the most toys wins." Skyrocketing rates of state murder
known as capital punishment. The lingering threat of
nuclear annihilation.

The world cannot save itself. And despite the fact
that so many churches in comfortable middle- and
upper-class circumstances now so proclaim it, the gospel heralding God's kingdom is not focused on the inner serenity of materially comfortable individuals. The
world needs so much more than that. And the kingdom of God is so much grander, so much more excit-
ing and challenging than that.

This is something an odd German pastor and some-time politician named Christoph Blumhardt knew very well. And this is why I have read the words of Blumhardt (and his father) with so much appreciation and encouragement. It is also why I have commended the Blumhardts to so many friends. (I have a box of Vernard Eller's *Thy Kingdom Come: A Blumhardt Reader,* from which I eagerly distribute copies to houseguests, hosts, workmates, and other potential converts.) It is, at last, why I consider it such a privilege to commend this wonderful new collection of some of Christoph Blumhardt's finest sermons.

Both Blumhardts were servants of the common folk. Their words are simple, straightforward, often bereft of the subtlety we rightly find in many great doctors of the church. Yet the Blumhardts rediscovered the king-dom of God, the victory of Jesus Christ narrated in the Bible, freshly and fully. They did not crowd it out of the precincts of earth exclusively into those of heaven, did not confine it to boundaries drawn by churches liberal or evangelical or Catholic, did not delay all ac-tual change of the world by it until Christ's return.

So if you read further into these pages you will find Christoph Blumhardt declaring the expansiveness of the kingdom: "When I await the Lord, my waiting is for the whole world, of which I am a part." You will find him railing against the privatistic reduction of the kingdom's power to individual salvation: "We have been much more concerned with being saved than with seeing the kingdom of God. If we want our salvation first, and then the kingdom of God, there will never be any light on earth. No! We will not think of our salvation. We will not seek our own good first! We want to be servants! We want to seek God's salvation, God's glory, God's kingdom!" You will find his bracing expectation that the world will change, however fitfully and incompletely, through the witness of God's people: "Today we cry, 'Oh, to be saved! Oh, to be saved!' But God says, 'I do not need you in heaven, I have enough saved ones here. I need workers, people who get things done on earth. First serve me there.' If we Christians simply relate all the words of scripture to our precious little selves without stopping to consider whether the conditions of our life and of our world are right – then it is our fault if nothing new breaks into our lives."

Blessedly, and surely partly through the direct and indirect influence of the Blumhardts, we live in a day when a host of biblical scholars and theologians are reading the Bible anew and appreciating both the centrality of the kingdom to the gospel, and the full-orbed social, political, and cultural (as well as "private" and "personal") inbreaking impact of that kingdom. This is in many ways a more Jewish reading of Scripture – and remember, Jesus and his apostles were Jews. In the early days of the church, non-Christianized Jews argued quite legitimately that if the world has not been changed, then the genuine Messiah has not come. After all, the prophets Isaiah, Jeremiah, and others said that with the kingdom's advent would come the cessation of war, the routing of famine and pestilence, the end of enmity between humanity and the rest of creation.

True enough, now as in the early days of the church there are still wars, hunger, sickness, and wild beasts. But the apostles and fathers of the church did not, as many Christians today are wont, reject the Jewish premise and utterly spiritualize the kingdom. Instead, on the one hand they recognized and admitted that the kingdom had not yet come in its fullness and finality, and would not until the return of Christ. And on the other hand, to cite just one contemporary scholar, Gerhard Lohfink, they proclaimed that "the Messiah has come and that the world has in fact changed. It has been transformed *in the Messiah's people,* which lives in accord with the law of Christ." Or, to resort again to the exhilarating words of Christoph Blumhardt:

> When Jesus speaks, it is a social matter, a matter for humanity. What Jesus did was to found the cause of God on earth, in order to establish a new society which finally is to include all nations – in contrast to the societies we have made, societies where not

even true families can be formed; where fathers do not know how to care for their children; where friendships are formed and torn apart; in short, where everyone lives in heartache. Faced with this wretched social order, Jesus wants to build a new one. His word to us is this: "You belong to God and not to these man-made societies."

Now that is a glorious and pulse-quickening vision, beckoning us to an adventure worth a lifetime's dedication and commitment. In focusing on the salvation of "our precious little selves," we have rendered the gospel so small, made God's kingdom so puny. Christoph Blumhardt, in plain language vibrant with eloquence only because it is so Spirit-filled, reminds us that personal peace, though not a bad thing, is merely the wrapping paper and not the magnificent gift itself. Dare I, dare we, dare the church on behalf of the world, pray for a confidence in the kingdom as vital and comprehensive as this man's?

It is frightening. It would change us and would once again, as in the days when the Word (and thus the kingdom) became flesh, "turn the world upside down" (Acts 17:6).

God grant us the courage so to pray and wait, and in the action of our waiting, so to live.

Rodney Clapp
Lent, 1998

Introduction

Christoph Friedrich Blumhardt (1842–1919) was an original. There is no one quite like him. He is not easy to characterize – theologically, politically, or otherwise. He was at home nowhere – he belonged neither to church circles nor to secular ones. He was an embarrassment to Christians and non-Christians alike. He seemed to challenge and disconcert everyone. And yet he possessed a strange confidence in God's history; a confidence that inspired hope in many, and continues to do so even today.

Blumhardt possessed no theories and certainly no "theology." Without founding a school or wanting to attract disciples, he pointed in a direction that had a striking influence on those who came after him. He was behind two movements that accepted him as one of their forerunners without having any direct contact with them: Religious Socialism (in Switzerland and Germany) and Dialectical ("Crisis") Theology. His ideas had seminal influence on Leonhard Ragaz, Karl Barth, Emil Brunner, and Dietrich Bonhoeffer, and more recently on Harvey Cox, Jacques Ellul, and Jürgen Moltmann – theological giants among whom he would most certainly feel a stranger.

There are movements today like the rapidly growing

Vineyard Church that seize Blumhardt and his father as two of their most cherished witnesses – forerunners of today's outbreak of signs and wonders. In Blumhardt we have a demonstration of kingdom power combined with repentance, a power that has become commonplace among many charismatic and Pentecostal movements.

Despite his legacy, Blumhardt is relatively unknown – especially in America. This is, for instance, his only book currently in print in English. True, efforts have been made in the past to make him better known. But without much effect. Unlike some of his contemporaries – Charles Finney or William Booth, for example – Blumhardt is known only to a very few.

In a piece written for *The Christian Century* in 1969, Vernard Eller suggests that part of the reason for Blumhardt's obscurity is that his message was neither literary nor scholarly enough to quote from. In his book *Thy Kingdom Come: A Blumhardt Reader* (Eerdmans, 1980), Eller attempted to rectify this. Unfortunately, the book never received much attention.

But there is perhaps a more basic reason. To begin with, Blumhardt's life was a provocation. He also expressed his ideas in impressive and unconventional phrases. His message excited both shock and indignation, for it went against the currents of both the church and the world. He represented something quite different from what we generally understand by Christianity. As Johannes Harder once wrote, "Anyone who wants to fit Blumhardt into the history of theology might place him into an appendix to Gottfried Arnold's *History of Heresy.*"

It was Blumhardt's conviction that the greatest of all dangers to human progress was "Christianity" – Sunday religion that separated material existence from the spiritual and that erected rituals and practices of self-seeking, self-satisfying, other-worldly piousness instead of practical works of righteousness.

Blumhardt didn't care about matters of religion and church, of worship services and dogma, not even of inner peace and personal redemption. For him, faith was a matter of the coming of God's kingdom, of God's victory over darkness and death here and now. His vision of God's righteousness on earth was an unconditional and all-embracing one: God's love reconciles the world, liberates suffering, heals economic and social need – in short, it renews the earth.

To many people, Blumhardt's message sounded dangerously worldly, even irreverent. In fact, the established church of his day retaliated by casting suspicion on him, and slandering and maligning him. His message touched a nerve that is still raw today.

Blumhardt's aim, however, was never to attack. What ruled his whole thinking was the kingdom of God – the creative reign of Christ's peace and justice on earth.

This kingdom is neither a formal constitution nor an ideal. It is a movement that belongs to the future but impinges upon the present. It is humankind's truest history, and will be demonstrably victorious in the end. It confronts everything that has ever been thought, planned, or built; it opposes all institutions, monuments, and ideologies. It always seeks the different, the new, and encompasses the whole of life.

Such a broad view of God's redemptive work pushes hard against the boundaries of traditional Christianity. And this could well be the real reason why Blumhardt's thought, though seminally forceful among an important few, has never had broad appeal.

We will return to this theme of the kingdom. Before we do, however, we must understand how concrete, how living this reign of God was for Blumhardt. Blumhardt was no visionary. His thought grew from his experience, not from theology. God's kingdom was something living for him, not an abstraction. It filled his being with the vividness of direct personal experience.

To appreciate this one must turn to Blumhardt's father, Johann Christoph (1805–1880). Blumhardt's father was the minister of Möttlingen, a small town at the edge of the Black Forest. His work followed the same course as that of any rural pastor until he came in touch with a girl by the name of Gottliebin Dittus. Gottliebin suffered from an illness perhaps similar to demonic possession as described in the New Testament. For months Father Blumhardt watched with distress the increasing suffering and torment of this young woman. Feeling something dark at work in her, he finally took up the fight with the power of darkness. In the year in which his son Christoph was born, in 1842, he exclaimed: "We have seen enough of what the devil can do. Let us now see the power of the Lord Jesus." The fight against the demonic stronghold commenced and lasted two years. The dark power was finally broken and conquered, and the evil spirit driven out. Gottliebin was completely healed of all bodily and spiritual misery. The fight ended in victory with the words from her lips, "Jesus is victor! Jesus is victor!"

As a consequence of this victory a movement of repentance swelled, taking hold of Blumhardt's whole parish and extending to the neighboring towns and villages. From all sides people streamed to Father Blumhardt. The inbreaking of kingdom power transformed the entire village of Möttlingen. There were healings, confessions, conversions. Marriages were saved, enemies reconciled. A strange new manifestation of God's world took sway. From this time on, Father Blumhardt's rallying cry was "Jesus is victor!" It was in this strangely moved world that his son Christoph grew up.

For a number of reasons, opposition to Blumhardt's father gradually increased, particularly from other ministers and the state church authorities. Local clergy complained about the flight of their parishioners to Blumhardt. Soon the parsonage could not accommodate the numbers of people who were beginning to stream to him. He thus began to look for a place where there would be both more room and greater freedom. When Christoph was only ten, the family moved to Bad Boll, a complex of large buildings which had been developed as a spa around a sulfur water spring. This became a kind of retreat center, a place to which people could have recourse for periods of rest, meditation, study, and pastoral counsel – and a place where the father Blumhardt was free to operate according to God's leading.

The father Blumhardt spent the rest of his life in Bad Boll, and his son spent most of his adult life there. Thousands came to his father to experience the healing and strengthening of Christ's victory. This was Christoph's experience and his foundation. It is no surprise that the amazing experiences of his father engraved themselves indelibly upon Christoph's soul, compelling him forward along the same path.

In Bad Boll, the young Christoph found himself in the midst of a stream of people seeking help, coming from all classes, nationalities, and countries, and in the midst of the work of his father's constant, fervent

struggle for God's kingdom. In time he felt called to
the ministry himself, and after some years he was per-
mitted to support his father as an assistant. When his
father called him to Bad Boll as his helper, however, he
only wanted to make himself useful around the house
in the most menial ways; perhaps as a cook's helper.
For some reason he lacked his father's certainty. He had
yet to personally take up the fight that his father had
undertaken. But the death of Gottliebin Dittus, in 1872,
became a turning point for him and the entire household at Bad Boll. It drove everybody to a fresh experience of deep repentance, releasing in Christoph a renewed confidence in God's call. His father's last words,
spoken on his deathbed in 1880, commissioned Christoph to carry on: "I give you a blessing for victory."

Blumhardt undertook his father's work in deep hu-
mility. Equipped with his father's spirit, he too experienced great demonstrations of the Spirit and of power.
But Blumhardt could not stop at these happenings. For
him, the gospel proved to be full of life, and this bade
him to go other ways than his father. It was not long
before he was out of the church entirely. His exit was in
part due to his own wish, and in part due to the wish of
the church authorities. Eventually, and with much
struggle, he broke with all the outward forms of church
life, clerical robe and all. Theology, religious factions,

and even the different confessions all meant the same thing to him: all were based on human symbols, arrangements, and pride – the flesh.

Blumhardt also became frustrated with the constant attention people placed on healing. As happened in the time of Jesus, "miracles" became the main thing for many people in Bad Boll. He consciously fought against this. He was determined to keep Bad Boll from becoming an institution for faith healing. "There is a lie that turns everything in the direction of exploiting the mercy and grace of God in such a way that the Savior then becomes our servant," he once wrote in a letter to someone asking for his help. For Blumhardt, the conquest of sickness was subservient to God's kingdom. "To be cleansed is more important than to be healed."

It wasn't until Blumhardt was causing a sensation on his mission journeys in Germany and Switzerland that he came to seriously question the whole direction of his work. After his return from Berlin in March of 1888, Blumhardt not only retired from his public preaching activity, but his healing of sickness also receded. He felt misunderstood by those who flocked to him: "I am terribly sorry that people say I am a famous preacher. I don't want to be a speaker before you. I am no speaker at all, nor do I want to be one. I want to be a man of experience. I do not merely want these things to be spoken about. I want to stand before you as a witness!"

He believed that possessing a heart for God's cause was the surest sign of God's kingdom, not numbers or healings. For Blumhardt, God's love carried not only the burdens of individuals, but also of those bound in the shackles of poverty. In time, Blumhardt's whole heart was opened to the wretchedness and sin of the world. A burning desire arose within him for God's justice, and this led him to a deeper awareness of the misery, the poverty, and the inequity around him in Germany and in the world. Because of this, he sensed God's voice in the new movements of protest and revolt – against injustice, capitalism, against war. He saw longings of hope in the great social movements of his day. "The struggle of millions in our time is not a coincidence. It is related to the struggle of the apostles – these are signs of our Lord Jesus Christ."

In the prophets, even pagan peoples like the Assyrians, Babylonians, and Persians, and heathen kings like Nebuchadnezzar and Cyrus were in God's service. Blumhardt began to wonder why a socialist movement that aimed to help humanity couldn't also serve as an instrument in God's hand. Despite socialism's foibles and shortcomings, Blumhardt believed that Christ was surely hidden in it.

Still following in his father's footsteps, Blumhardt concerned himself more and more with the reality of present-day society. He finally left the "conventicle" in

Bad Boll and went into the streets to support the labor movement, which was making itself heard. Bad Boll would cease to be a "place of sermons," in order to become a "place for true life." Blumhardt stood virtually alone among people in the churches in this feeling for the need of the masses. When he joined the Social Democrats (and acted as their elected representative to the Württemberg parliament from 1900–1906) it was as though he was under banishment. He was asked to renounce his position as a pastor in the state of Württemberg. The organized churches marked him as an outcast. Blumhardt accepted this as a freeing: "State and church are no soil for the fire of God."

However, Blumhardt's outlook did not hang on the hopes of socialism alone in these years. All that moved in the masses, as well as in nature, came under the light of the kingdom. Blumhardt saw plenty of signs in science and the economy that could be received as messengers of a future epoch of tremendous change. He endeavored to read the signs of the times and was convinced that Christ wanted to break into the world situation to free those gripped by its degenerative powers.

Blumhardt's spiritual radicalism meant a social commitment. If God's kingdom penetrated all of creation, then so should our witness: "The kingdom of God is taking on colossal dimensions these days. We have to come out of our little rooms, out of our isolation. The kingdom comes into the streets, where the poorest live, the outcasts, the miserable. There the kingdom of God comes. It extends into the heavens and into hell, and to all peoples."

This kingdom is anything but religion. It is certainly not Christianity. Blumhardt believed that the prophets and Jesus wanted a new world; the rulership of God over all reality. In his view, heaven and personal salvation were not the aim of history. God is not concerned that we get into heaven; rather, heaven must come down to earth. "Many people long and yearn for heaven; they stretch out toward heaven. I would like to tell them: Let your minds reach to the heights that we can already perceive on earth. Down here is where Jesus appeared, not above in the invisible world. Here on earth he wants to appear again and again. Here on earth we may find him."

The idea that God is only in heaven and that the application of the gospel was only for the inner life was disastrous, according to Blumhardt. Not our blessedness first, but the kingdom of God. Not our profit (here or hereafter), but the honor of God. Or, as Leonhard Ragaz once put it in summarizing Blumhardt's thought, "From religion to God's kingdom, from the church to a redeemed world, from *me* to God." This all-encompassing vision ultimately led Blumhardt back to Bad Boll.

Blumhardt was never really a politician. Only by circumstance was he forced into formally joining the

Social Democratic party. Originally he did not even want to become a regular party member. Though received with open arms, in the long run he did not find the party to be ground in which a witness to the gospel could have full effect. He said: "The social movement as we see it today still belongs to the world that will pass. It does not contain the fellowship of men as it will one day come through God's spirit." Therefore, after his first term he was led back through a long, serious illness into the peace of Bad Boll. In 1917 Blumhardt suffered a stroke; he died peacefully two years later, on August 2, 1919.

Blumhardt was unrelenting in his fight against churchiness – against dogmatic, institutional, and pious Christianity – precisely because he was consumed with the coming reign of God. For him, this gospel of the kingdom opposes all religiousness. It demands a fundamental change, a revolution of life. Jesus was no teacher of doctrine, no divine example of heavenly virtue. He both taught and lived out God's new world. He was the initiator of a new age; a new society where God's justice and healing is established. His final coming is but a completion of what he has begun. His death sealed the fight against the powers of the old world, his resurrection was the victorious dawning of the new world – the beginning of a new epoch in history, a new morning of creation – and his return is its consummation.

Despite misunderstanding, despite much opposition, Blumhardt was a man of unwavering hope. For him the gospel was the good tidings of the future day of Christ. "The Savior is coming!" What mattered to him, in the end, was *God's* coming kingdom; a reality not to be confused with any human philosophy of progress. This kingdom is not self-created human betterment. It is certainly for the world, but not from it. Neither political endeavors nor Christian piety will bring in the kingdom. "Not through our faith, through our prayer nor our piety, but through the deeds of God will the future city of God be revealed."

This did not mean that those who await Christ's future should just place their hands in their laps and do nothing. Far from it! The powers of the future are already here, and God's people must live in these powers, responding to them, letting them grow. In this sense, according to Blumhardt, our deepest service is to wait for God's action. We must both wait for and hurry toward the coming of Christ. In spite of all necessary activity on our part, we must trust that in our strivings God's kingdom will overcome every obstacle.

From this expectation, Blumhardt believed that a people of Christ should gradually be gathered – gathered to wait, gathered to live together in the powers of the future. "God always wants to have a place, a community, which belongs genuinely to him, so that God's being can dwell there. God needs such a place from where he can work for the rest of the world. There must be a place on the earth, a Zion, from where the sun of God's kingdom shines forth." In Christ, the old creation is to yield to the new as the night yields to the dawning day.

This "waiting" involves a kind of double movement. As Vernard Eller explains: "We are to give ourselves completely to the cause of the kingdom, do everything in our power to help the world toward that goal. At the same time, however, we are to remain calm and patient, unperturbed even if our efforts show no signs of success. Far from being inactivity, this sort of waiting is itself a tremendously strong and creative action in the very hastening of the kingdom."

As one hears the message of Blumhardt, there is a sense that truth is being served in a timeless way. Perhaps this is because for Blumhardt, Jesus is rising now; Jesus is victorious now; the kingdom of God is breaking in now! The fabric of God's kingdom-vision spans time and brings together unlikely witnesses who have been blessed to see the Real despite the illusions of their day.

One such visionary of our time has been Archbishop Oscar Romero, whose death from an assassin's bullet in 1980 crowned a life of service to El Salvador's poor. Like Blumhardt, Romero had the grace to see what God is doing now. What Romero expresses poetically in his prayer, Blumhardt expresses in passionate prose. The kingdom that Romero challenges his people to embrace is the same rulership that so powerfully gripped Blumhardt. When one sets the prayer of the modern martyr side by side with the passion of one so sorely misunderstood, there steps out in stark relief a timeless and united Christian vision. The kingdom of God is at hand. We must fight *and* wait for it in the singular act of concrete expectation.

Hence our choice of a prayer attributed to Oscar Romero (see p. xxx) as the leitmotif for this collection of essays. In one sense, what we have here is but a sampler. Neither the breadth of Blumhardt's thought nor the depth of Romero's prayer can be fully expressed in a short volume like this one. However, we hope that the spirit and longing of each can. Blumhardt was gripped by the reality of the coming of God's kingdom on this earth, here and now. Romero understood, like Blumhardt, that this kingdom was yet beyond our efforts, always lying beyond us. For both, however, God's kingdom ignited a burning expectancy of living faith; a faith that both works and waits, helps God and hopes in him. May Blumhardt's vision and Romero's prayer inspire in the reader such deeds of hope. At the dawn of a new millennium, we surely need more of them.

Charles Moore
May 1998

The Prayer
of Oscar Romero

It helps now and then to step back and take the
   long view.
The kingdom is not only beyond our efforts; it is
   even beyond our vision.
We accomplish in our lifetime only a tiny fraction
   of the magnificent enterprise that is God's work.
Nothing we do is complete, which is another way
   of saying that the kingdom always lies beyond us.
No statement says all that could be said.
No prayer fully expresses our faith.
No confession brings perfection, no pastoral visit
   brings wholeness.
No program accomplishes the church's mission.
No set of goals and objectives includes everything.

This is what we are about:
We plant the seeds that one day will grow.
We water seeds already planted, knowing that they
   hold future promise.
We lay foundations that will need further
   development.

We provide yeast that produces effects far beyond
our capabilities.

We cannot do everything, and there is a sense of
liberation in realizing that.

This enables us to do something and to do it very
well.

It may be incomplete, but it is a beginning, a step
along the way, an opportunity for
God's grace to enter and do the rest.

We may never see the end results, but that is the
difference between the master builder and the
worker.

We are workers, not master builders – ministers,
not messiahs.

We are prophets of a future not our own.

Amen.

Step back and take

the long view. **Oscar Romero**

Seek first God's kingdom
and his righteousness,
and all these things will
be given to you as well.

Matthew 6:33

1

Seeking the Kingdom

The history of Jesus' life is the history of God's kingdom then and now. Some people have been shaken and gripped by this. But for many people today the kingdom of God has drifted out of sight. People are stirred by many issues; the outward life makes great demands on them. More than at any other time, it would seem, man raises himself powerfully in his human search and progress. It is as though the whole world wanted to offer us its strength, saying, "Use me. Become great, become strong, become rich, creative, active – take everything into your own hands!" Powers that earlier times hardly dreamed of are now opened

3

up for us. Everyone finds himself in a position to make use of these new inventions and these new powers for his own purposes. Our whole society seems to depend on this. If we were to shut our eyes to these things, we would lag behind and finally perish in our earthly life. There is a spirit of intellectual accomplishment that pushes the concern for God's kingdom to the side.

A tremendous misunderstanding has come about with regard to God's kingdom. Much has been said about the church. Much has been said about the teachings that are preserved in the church, about the various denominations that have become a sacred good within the body of Christianity. Too much emphasis has been placed on forms by which we express ourselves as Christians. Thus today we cannot deny that many people no longer really find the living qualities that our Father in heaven wanted to give us in Jesus Christ. They have neither seen nor experienced the life that comes from God, and so they are in a fix. On the one hand they cannot deny that they too need God, God's word, God's revelation, in their hearts. On the other hand they no longer quite believe in the means through which God's word is being proclaimed, and thus many of them no longer know what to do with themselves in regard to God's kingdom. Their hearts hunger and thirst; they are aware that something of God's eternity and truth should be revealed in us, but they don't quite know what to do about it.

Because of all this we must begin to speak of God's kingdom in a new way. In spite of present-day conditions where much of the church and of Christian fellowship is almost dead, we can speak of God's kingdom to men and women of our time. The kingdom of God is and was and will be the rulership of justice, of order, of power, of authority, of all that is of God, over creation. This is what moves those of us who seek, and this must come more fully into being. And unless our lives are molded according to this rulership, we shall always remain dissatisfied. We may enjoy modern conveniences, but the reality of eternal things will be smothered unless the reign of God's truth and justice dawns as the light of life.

For many people, God's kingdom has drifted out of sight.

Yet this very fact causes great discord as soon as it is pointed out. Millions of people are "Christians" in all peace and comfort from their childhood on until they are laid in the grave. They are satisfied with what is said about God, and it does not make them feel uncomfortable in any way. Religion is taken as part of one's life; one accepts it such as it is. This causes no conflict – at the most an argument here or there about the interpretation of this or that teaching, but these arguments are futile. A new conflict arises as soon as we feel urged to

Jesus lives and acts; he is not an empty word or a mere teaching.

proclaim the kingdom of God as something living. And this is what I want to do today. I don't just want to edify you. I want to proclaim to you what God has put into my heart: God's kingdom is a living reality, a rulership that impacts the here and now and even today is at hand – closer at hand than we may think. The intervention of the living God is more powerful today than many believe. God wants to manifest himself as the one who is something and who *does* something now. He alone is the one with whom we should joyfully concern ourselves.

In speaking of God's kingdom, we proclaim that Jesus Christ is not dead. He is not merely someone who appeared two thousand years ago, to be viewed as a personality of the past about whom we retain certain recollections and teachings. No, just as Jesus lived two thousand years ago, he lives today. He wants to triumph in our midst for the honor of God. He wants to live among us so that our reverence for the Father in heaven may grow and deepen. We must come before God and in the weakness and poverty of our natures raise our eyes to him with a sigh in our hearts, saying, "My Father, my Father, I too want to be your child!" Then we may believe with life-giving strength: Jesus lives, he will help me, he is victor. Whoever I may be, his name can be sanctified in me and his rulership can enter in, so that his will may be done in me just as it is done in heaven!

I wish, my friends, that I could place in your hearts the living power of God. I wish that I could help you understand that this power makes us completely new. It can overcome much of our misery, even in our physical life. God's living power seeks us out and wants to show us – despite the entanglements of life – clear, true values that can ennoble us.

In the realm of our own human nature, however, there is more resistance to God's truth than people believe. And in human society, in all the influences to which we are exposed, there lies a grave hindrance to the living power of Christ, and this hindrance is also greater than people suspect. Often I find that when I speak of God, of Christ, and of the Holy Spirit, everyone agrees with me. Nobody gets annoyed. The conflict begins, however, as soon as I take a firm stand and say, "I have experienced who Jesus is. I have looked into the living power, into the kingdom of our God, which even today wants to take hold of us. I tell you that even now the truth and the life-power of our God is at work. I declare to you that even now the truth of God's kingdom comes visibly to this earth. We do not have to wait until we lay ourselves down to die and be buried. Here and now we can hear with our ears, see with our eyes, who Jesus is, who the life-giving spirit is. It is the same today as at the time of the apostles. It is not a question of this or that church, of this or that teaching, but only of Jesus Christ himself (John 14:6). We have to come to terms with him!"

For me this is the one and only direction. Yet if I say this, people react and argue. "Who is this arrogant person? How can anyone say such things today? Aren't the Bible and the existing denominations enough for us? This is superstition and exaggeration!" So there is a conflict, but it kindles a light in many hearts, a light of hope, a light of strength, a light from the heights beyond this earth. For nothing can give us more strength than the certainty that Jesus lives and acts and that he is not an empty word or a mere teaching. Nothing gives more strength than the knowledge that Jesus is in our midst (Matt. 18:20). We must believe this, so that his life may become true in us, so that his spirit may purify us.

What then does it mean to believe? There is much dispute about belief; but woe to us and our arguments about faith! Isn't it something quite simple, something every child can understand? My friends, if Jesus truly lives, if he is king of kings, then you must no longer take anything into your own hands. You must deny yourself in all things that are God's. You must be a dying person, one who in things of God says, "I can do nothing. None but Jesus has the right to show us divine matters!" In this way alone do we honor this king.

If God's kingdom is important to you, then you need not think you have to be anything important. Rather, you should place yourself at Jesus' feet, thinking, I am a weak human being, but Jesus lives, Jesus is victor. I will give myself to him, and I will turn everything over to him so that nothing can rule over me but he alone.

This is faith. If we believe in Jesus Christ, then we must stand firm. It will be of no use to you to have heard someone speak, to believe in a doctrine, or to sacrifice yourselves to some good cause. All this will be of no avail.

Therefore I would like to call out into the world, "Die, that Jesus may live!" (Gal. 2:20) In other words, do not attach any importance to what is false, to what is opposed to truth. Jesus Christ is the Lord. Raise your fists against all that comes from the flesh, from the deceitfulness of your own thinking. What is false shall be called false. Do it for the sake of God your Savior! What is wrong shall die and die again, and die so that it no longer counts for anything. Then we shall be amazed at how much is possible through his rulership.

If God's kingdom is important to you, then you do not have to be anything important.

The kingdom
is not only beyond
our efforts; it is even
beyond our vision.

Oscar
Romero

And he who sat
upon the throne said,
"Behold, I make all things new."
Also he said, "Write this,
for these words are
trustworthy and true."

Revelation 21:5

2

I Make All Things New

The greatest word that crowns all others is this: "I make all things new!" This is of special support and comfort when we realize how quickly everything passes away and becomes dust and ashes. All things new! God cannot tolerate what is corrupt and destructive but wants to change it. Of course we enter into new life only through repentance (Acts 2:37–38). Sadly, many people think of all sorts of things around them that need to change and not at all of themselves. Or they would like to have only certain things change so as to be able to carry on more comfortably. We should be deeply humiliated to realize that there actually is nothing that must not also become new, especially ourselves. If I were to take a close look at each one of you – all of you must become new!

This is how things are, my friends. A darkness has come over Christianity in regard to this very matter of renewal. We are so easily contented and so quickly satisfied with a Christianity that makes us only a little more decent. That is all people want. And yet if one takes a look at it one must say, "This cannot be all." Not just a little taste of something new, but all things new, in yourselves first and foremost. How long have we been sitting around here; how long are we being preached to; how long have we let ourselves be admonished again and again! And still there is no breakthrough to something new. It could make one die of grief to see how little has actually happened. So much that is new lies before us, and still there are so few results; it is always at our doorstep, and still it will not come in.

This could depress us very much. Instead, it should unite us in repentance. But why then don't we turn around? Why do we not receive strength against sin? Why is it that so little happens? "Jesus Christ, our Savior, have mercy on us!" Shouldn't this be our cry?

There are so many proud Christians; yet they have nothing to be proud of. They are intoxicated by their piety, and each one thinks that he is the one, that he's got it, that his group is it. This is true for each one of us. Unless this changes, we will perish; we might as well join in the stream of death. Then you will see how in all their customs and practices people trudge along at the same old monotonous pace, till finally they are laid in the grave. Dirt is thrown over them, and everyone goes back home and continues living just as dully and superficially as before.

Therefore, turn to God! God does not say, "Perhaps, if possible, under certain circumstances, I will make things new; I have to think it over." He says straight out, "I make all things new." This promise belongs to our time. It is ready for anyone who wants to become new, who is ready to give up his possessions, who does not push his own person into the foreground and does not love his own life. Just try it! Go completely into repentance and then fully into faith. Even if only a few become new, it will still be something. And finally all things shall be made new.

In facing the judgments that have come upon the earth and that may yet come over us, we can lean upon this promise in faith. You know very well how things are. Murderous weapons are ready. The powers of darkness have risen and want to drive things to the point where the earth becomes a pool of blood. Must there be war and rumors of war forever? If we cannot pray

If we cannot pray for God to hold back warring armies, then it is a mockery to believe he can make all things new.

for the time to come when God's almighty arm will hold back warring armies, then it is a mockery to believe that God makes all things new.

Every family must be prepared to have their peace suddenly disturbed.

Of course if everything is to be made new, then something must break in, not coming from us but from heaven. A new deed of God must happen; something living and real from Jesus must break into the physical world. It must become visible enough to show that the almighty God really *is*, and in such a way that he will not let himself be pushed to the side. But too many people just don't believe that God does something from above. They might say, "He guides the destinies of the nations," but then everything gets labeled as being from God, even when it is the Evil One who does it. The time must come when we pray that the threatening dangers to God's creation will be averted and our prayer will be answered.

There are many things that threaten us. Even if war does not break out, millions of people lose their lives all over the world through all kinds of trials: storms, landslides, explosions, earthquakes, epidemics, all kinds of accidents. At the same time there is an enormous amount of sickness of body and soul. How much sighing there still is in hospitals, how much misery in the mental institutions. And how many are being killed, some slowly, through envy, through hatred, through maliciousness of people towards each other. Just think of all the people murdered in one year. It doesn't even take guns; people are perishing anyway.

Every family must be prepared for something to happen suddenly that will disturb its peace. Then we have to believe and pray that the judgments may be turned away. If God keeps his word, we can stand up against anything, especially if we ourselves are already living in what is new (1 John 5:3–5). Arise and go to meet what is new. Pray for it. Beg for it. The whole world will yet be renewed through the almighty power of God.

This alone is what Jesus Christ wants. For this reason he is the firstborn from the dead. For this Christ was born, for this he died and arose, for this he is sitting at God's right hand. Go to meet this renewal so that it may come! This is what we must believe; this is how we must see what is before us.

When the divine comes, look out. Then we shall pass through judgment, through fire. Then we shall have to be purified, to become gold, not wood. Then we must become completely true, just as what is in heaven is true, just as the Lord Jesus is whole and true and all the angels are true and God himself is true (Heb. 6:13–18). So you also must become true. This is what new means. And this new thing is not something unheard-of. It is at our doorstep; it is already on the earth. Whoever has had a little to do with the Savior always sees something new.

Jesus said, "I am the way, the truth, and the life."

What is at stake is the truth. This truth must become a new reality. It is not a matter of new teachings, new laws, new institutions. True, Christianity has made many teachings and laws and institutions in the name of Jesus. Yet this is not the truth Christ speaks of. The truth to which we must open our ears is the new reality the Son of Man brings to the world. It is the message that God now creates a new reality on the earth, beginning among his people, and later in the whole creation. Heaven and earth will be renewed in this new reality (2 Pet. 3:12–13).

Too many of us live in the old reality, which completely occupies all our senses. It is the old story of perishing, of wasting away, and behind it lies a mighty darkness: death. We live and die. Nature lives and then dies. Sin enters into life. There are failures; people go wrong. In Jesus, however, a new reality appears, a reality that is opposed to the world's history. Something new begins alongside the old.

The old reality does not suddenly disappear; it continues alongside the new. Yet in Jesus a new history begins, a new working of God (1 John 2:8). True, God has always been present in the old, and the Spirit has worked upon it throughout the ages. But now, yes now, something new has begun in Christ. God has meant it to be like that from the very beginning, but death still has its dominion. Even in the lives of the believing, death makes itself felt. This death was particularly strong when Jesus appeared, this darkness caused by the law, this deadliness of human teachings. Death's power is so strong that Jesus had to struggle greatly in order to make people see that in him something completely different had come, a new history.

What use is our faith if things keep going in the same old ruts?

This history is to be revealed in each individual person. It must become evident in you, in me, in all of us. Now something new is possible. Unless we place ourselves within this truth, we can accomplish nothing. This is no dogma; it is not just a new word. It is the Word that has power. It is the living person of Jesus Christ, in whom humanity's new history dawns and in whom history culminates. Are you living in the reality of Jesus Christ? Have you placed yourself under the authority that has been given to him for you and for all people? Can you really grasp this? Can you accept it? Can you take it into your life? Can you let it guide your whole life, even in the midst of the deepest suffering?

Unless you do this you have no business striving after the kingdom of God. For what is God's kingdom anyway? Certainly not Christian causes or institutions. God's kingdom is the power of God. It is the rulership of God. God's kingdom is the revelation of the divine life here on earth, the birth of new hearts, new minds, new feelings, new possibilities. This is God's kingdom. Yet who can grasp what God's rule means? Who can grasp what God is at all?

To fully understand this we must acknowledge that Jesus has come from God. He is the light that shines throughout the centuries (John 1:9). Only by him can it be said, "Can any of you convict me of sin?" Jesus has come from God to triumph over death. Jesus Christ has come into our midst as one of us so that death can be conquered. He has laid the foundation for a completely new life, a new order. In him we can become completely different men and women in the very depth of our beings.

This is the power, the true nature of God's kingdom. Of what use is our Christianity if we keep falling back into death and if darkness continues to dominate our lives? What use is our faith in Christ if everything goes on in the old ruts? We are in a bad way if the power of sin continues to work in us. Then our Christianity, our belief and worship of God, is of little value. Facts must become visible, facts of life, of new life, new strength, new joy. We no longer live under the rulership of death, nor under its power of sin. We live in the reality of the true life that comes from God.

Two currents are now running alongside and in opposite directions, one to the other. Sin wants to rule. It wants to reach its goal; it wants to wreak destruction wherever it can. Against this current, however, runs the movement of Jesus Christ, the Prince of Life. He leads us into something completely beyond ourselves. Even death can be overcome. Even if we still have to die, he promises, "Whoever believes in me shall not see death, even though he die." What greater promise could be said to us than this? If we can hear these words and realize them, then even the history of the nations will be renewed.

In Christ a new day has dawned. It has come into the past, and it will come into the future. It is the eternity of God. For Christ is the one who rose from the dead. And because he is risen, it is he alone who matters. We do not want to cling to what is human, not even to those who are religious or godly. Everything must come from the ruler, from Christ the Lord. He alone is victorious. He alone pierces through the powers of sin and death, both in the world and in our own hearts. No human being, no human movement can do it. Not even the best will achieve it. But there is a new possibility. God can rule the world again. This possibility must live in our hearts. Then the true Christ will be with us, he who came to make all things new.

We accomplish in
our lifetime only
a tiny fraction
of the magnificent
enterprise that is
God's work.

Oscar
Romero

Let us hold unswervingly to the hope
we profess, for he who promised is faithful.
And let us consider how we may spur
one another on toward love and good deeds…
Let us encourage one another – and all the
more as you see the Day approaching.

Hebrews 10:23–25

3

Get Busy and Wait!

Christ is the beginning and the end of God's kingdom. Therefore we can say with all confidence
and certainty, "The Savior will come again!" He is bound
to complete his work, and it is our task simply to be
servants until his return, to be in the service of him
who is coming. We are, as it were, to represent by our
lives the coming of Jesus Christ. We must not, therefore, be so concerned and active, or make such tremendous efforts, as though we were able to achieve the victory of good on this earth. This, of course, we are quite

incapable of doing. Only the Lord Jesus can bring it about, he who came a first time and is going to come again a second time. He will complete it – not we. If we are loyally and firmly set upon this – "He will come again" – then the gospel of the kingdom will become personal and living to us. We must never separate this gospel from Christ's person. Without his personal presence no talking about the gospel, no talking about his coming kingdom is of any value at all.

So we must be prepared for the coming of Jesus Christ, which is not only something in the future but a present reality in those who wait for it in their hearts. We are to be servants watching for his return. Not that we get everything nicely arranged for ourselves, but we can and we must postpone our main concerns until he comes.

His servants have a twofold task: they are to wait for him in the sense of being active and doing something, and they are to be stewards. The waiting for the Savior involves a personal relationship to him as to a living person, making the gospel living and relevant. There are many people who are always waiting for something new in Christianity, as if something could be achieved through a new faith or a new church. We leave all that alone. We hold fast to the promise of a personal Savior, whom God will send as he has sent him before. And we know that we as persons are quite unable to lead a faithful life unless our Savior is personally with us.

All our strength, all our intellect, and all our feelings, however living and active they may be, will all pass away. We are living in a time of dying (1 Cor. 7:31). We do not want to hide from it. Our powers are declining. Our thinking is becoming feeble, and all our emotions, however lively they may be, will pass away. The law of death envelops everything we do and think and feel. But now a law of life breaks into all this dying, and it is the Lord Jesus himself. He is the one who lives forever, who rose from the dead, who keeps in touch with us from the world beyond, who sends us the Spirit, so that in the midst of our dying we may live and may ever again receive something fresh and living through his gift, through his presence, through his coming.

Christ's coming is not for the end of time, but for the here and now.

Far from expecting his coming as something to be realized only at the end of time, we must have the vision of the coming Savior always here and now in our lives. Jesus will come again for sure. His Day is approaching, and in the meantime, as I experienced him once, so may I experience him again and again. As the gospel is life and consolation for me, it can come again. It disappears, but it returns. Jesus will never let you down. If he has once begun something within you, then that will always come again, and if you hold on to it, it will shine as a light for you so that you may be joyful even in the most bitter tribulation – yes, even right unto death (Phil. 1:6). Never let go of the thought, he will come again! For this makes you into a servant. His earthly life is by no means lost forever – no, his life on earth is being continued, and by directing our whole heart and all our senses to it, by waiting for him and receiving, we may become servants of his life on earth.

The whole world is embraced by God's love. No one is excluded, not even atheists.

Those who wait open their hearts to him when he comes and knocks (Rev. 3:20). Jesus is alive. No matter how sad things may be, and when we are grieving on the earth for the people we most love and who perhaps will be taken from us, our deepest longing must be for the coming of Christ. The Lord Jesus occupies the highest position (Col. 1:15–18). He is more important than anything else. And though we be surrounded by sickness, need, and death, none of this is important; none of this may fill our hearts. No. He, the living one, is coming! He is highest of all, and quite certainly he is coming! For this we want to live, for this we are ready to go through suffering and fear, for this we want to fight unto death: he is coming! This stands firm and certain for us, and in this light we want to live as long as we are on this earth.

Now the servant's task does not consist in merely waiting and doing nothing. Rather it is a matter of practicing stewardship. Good stewardship means looking after the servants, that is, those who are in our care. And if only our hearts and minds were big enough, I would say that all the people on earth are entrusted to our care (Gal. 6:9–10). The servants of Christ are to stretch out their hands to each other and to all people as they look toward the coming of the Savior. Many people think that Christ's second coming means a dreadful judgment, when unbelievers will be cast into hell and believers will be saved. No, when Jesus comes, he wants to find his servants prepared to receive him as a Savior, a helper who comes into the world not in order to judge and condemn, but rather to redeem and to make whole, because this is what God created him for. Ever since Jesus' first coming, the whole world is embraced by the love of God. No one is excluded, not even the atheists. They are all embraced by God's love, and, through us, they are God's household. They, too, can do something. We can see in our time how people are doing much good on the earth, so that lives are made easier. We meet with all sorts of kindness on earth, through people's help, through God's larger household that is in the care of his servants.

Woe to us, therefore, if we start to judge, if we condemn, if we abandon all hope for this world for which Jesus Christ has come, for which he suffered and died, for which he rose again, and for which he will truly come again.

So you must be a steward – not a lazy servant who simply waits, but a diligent steward. There is much to be done. All around you there are lives entrusted to your care, people with whom you have been led together. They are perhaps still very worldly: your own family, maybe, or perhaps your next door neighbor. We need to see even nations as "households of God" and love them as the Father in heaven loves them. Our goodwill and good wishes must go out to them, just as the Father in heaven does nothing but good to all people. "He causes his sun to rise on the evil and the good, and sends rain on the righteous and the unrighteous" (Matt. 5:45). We want to be concerned that powers of redemption may go out from the Savior to many, many people, even if we cannot understand it, even if we have to wait for a long time. But one day the doors will burst open. Hearts will be freed. And new peace and new joy will descend upon the earth.

I am frequently saddened to hear and see how so many people who call themselves Christians, and often even real Christians, cannot bring themselves to wish good to all people as they wish it for themselves. How few are filled with God's gift of forgiveness! Instead most set themselves apart by setting themselves above others. But if we are awaiting the Savior, then we are awaiting the forgiveness of the world's sins, not just our own (1 John 2:2).

Unless the urge to forgive, to want the Savior for all people, wells up in our hearts, we are not true servants. Although we might know of God's will toward love, toward mercy, toward forgiveness, we nevertheless fail to do his will because the love of God does not fully govern our lives. For this we will be punished. For if we do not stand fully in the love of God and in his forgiveness, if the eyes with which we look out into the world are not good and kind, if we cease to hold on to the others in love, then God will no longer hold on to us either, and we will find ourselves with the unbelievers, regardless of whether we have spoken pious words or not (Matt. 6:14–15). God is not interested in words but reality. And the actual reality of a Christian life consists in forgiveness and in wishing the whole world well, however grim it may look. Even if war or bloodshed comes, God is greater. He carries out his will. In the end, sin will cease. In the end, it is justice and truth and the love of God that will come to us.

We are waiting for the forgiveness of the world's sins, not just our own.

I cannot live for one single hour without thinking: Come, Lord Jesus! And if all of us together can come to thinking that thought – even when there is trouble in your home and in your heart – then we shall be as one, and it will be granted us to go on experiencing the powers of God as a witness to the coming one. The marvelous strength of God, such as we experience it in our sufferings and in our dying and really in everything, will become a testimony to the power of God. And to that end we remind ourselves that our Savior will return. Will it happen in the first watch or in the second? We do not ask how and when. At any moment he can enter. So let us partake of his divine power, and when we do we will have experienced something of his future.

There is not much value in any help we may receive from God outside the context of Jesus' coming. Among others, too, help is being rendered here and there. But where this has no relation to the coming Savior, it is of a merely passing character. When, however, it becomes related to Jesus Christ, the living one, he who is the beginning and the end, the Alpha and the Omega, who is and was and will come, then all help given to us becomes a part of eternity within us (Rev. 1:5–8). Then all such help that we receive makes us partakers of life eternal. For it is true: if we were to receive no help from God, our faith would be a poor thing.

But we can think of so many instances of his coming to us that it would be a real shame to say, "We have lost eternity; we cannot live with God." No, we are full of God's experience. Each day brings us something new, and we are allowed again and again to experience a great deal both in our own lives and in the lives of others, both in living and in dying. Yes, in dying we have seen much of the Savior's coming. The eyes of many people light up in their last hour because the Savior is on the way. Hence we feel full of comfort and joy, and unceasingly the refrain sings within us: Jesus will return; his Day is approaching! This song must surround and envelop our lives with its holy sounds so that we may gain increasing confidence and strength.

Let us be united and strong, for the task given us by Jesus is not too great for us. It is not beyond our strength to carry it through. We may make mistakes. Without knowing it, we may do things that deserve the hand of discipline. But God is merciful. He has made us his servants, and we want to remain his servants. For it is as his servants that we go to meet that great and mighty day of Christ. It will yet come to the whole world, the day of Christ, which will reveal to us the character of God and will fill us even more with eternal joy.

Nothing we do is complete, which is another way of saying that the kingdom always lies beyond us.

Oscar Romero

No one knows
about the day or hour,
not even the angels in heaven,
nor the Son, but only the Father.
As it was in the days of Noah,
so it will be at the coming of the
Son of Man…Therefore,
keep watch, because you do
not know on what day
your Lord will come.

Matthew 24:36–42

4

The Savior
Is Coming Now

any times the Savior calls out to us, "Watch! Be ready!" Here the call is especially to "watch for my coming, for my future!" With this call Jesus gives us a task. If we fulfill this task – to watch for his future – it is as though his future is coming into our present time. By our watching, God's future comes closer. It makes itself felt in our whole being, in our whole life. We cannot be swallowed up by the present, for we are bound to the future. We experience the future already in our time. Again and again new life is given; something opens up a way for us. And each time it is a piece of Jesus Christ's future.

Christ's future is not one single point in an absolute remoteness for which we are to wait, a mere coming event. This is hardly thinkable, for we would probably all go to sleep over it. Christ's future is now, or it is not at all. It must become an experience of every individual believer and for every congregation. God's deed through Jesus Christ must be your experience, today and tomorrow and every day.

The Savior is coming. He is not sitting on some celestial throne, resting somewhere in eternity, waiting for some particular time before he acts or a certain moment when he will suddenly plunge in. The coming of the Savior runs like a thread throughout history, through God's working in the world (Matt. 28:20). If this thread is not to break, then Jesus must always be coming. Often there are times of storm and thunder, of sorrow and suffering. Yet just when we think we cannot go on, new ways open before us. And there indeed will come a time when our waiting and watching, which has prepared the coming of the Lord, will be consummated.

I have fat volumes about the second coming of Christ and many people have told me to study them. Ah! I get so tired of this! Half of them I do not understand; I am too stupid. The authors make lengthy calculations and come to the most remarkable conclusions. One must really force oneself to understand these speculations. Again and again I have to think, O God, if this is your future coming, I don't get it! As far as I am concerned, all this can sink in the Rhine River, if I can only unite all people in just this one point: to expect something from God.

Christ's future is not merely a coming event. It is now, or it is not at all.

We should not talk too much about the second coming of Christ. We are not allowed to know how it is all going to happen. The interpretations of the book of Revelation spoil everything! They spoil everything. Take this idea to heart: When a person finds something of God in the Bible, he should act like a hamster: carry it quickly into his storeroom and not to the public. It is our quiet hope that he will come.

So then, watch. Watch, and be joyful. Even though fear may overcome you, watch. Something of the Savior's future will enter into your life. I have often experienced this in the way I have been led. There is always a way out. Even when I have felt I could not go

The Savior is coming. He is not sitting on some celestial throne.

on, God has opened a new way. Then one can continue. Then we have a portion of Christ's future in our midst. We depend on this coming of the Savior. All our thinking and living comes to life by the very fact that we are allowed to expect such great things, things that will finally lead to true life.

In our day there are many people who hope for the good. They refuse to believe that things will just go on and on as they are or that humanity will not reach any goal. Any hope for improvement, any belief that better days will come for the world, any striving towards better times, are a proof and a result of this one hope that we who believe firmly express by the words, "The Savior is coming!"

We should and can be ever alert and watchful. Jesus Christ's future has to become your personal experience. Whenever you experience protection and remarkable help, whenever you are led on new ways and see others being so led, you should think, "This is a piece of Christ's future." There is a special atmosphere in Christ's coming. All kinds of signs, all kinds of proofs of God's help, are visible. However poor we may be, however weak we may feel, we want to continue hoping and watching. A time will come when you will be allowed to act unhindered. That is a piece of Christ's future. All this remains a mystery of God.

The Savior is coming! He is on the way to you, to me, to us all, in all circumstances of our lives. Even when things are as they were in Noah's time, even if the whole world apparently is concerned with nothing but earthly things, with eating and drinking, with marrying and giving in marriage, we should not give up. We must be a living presence at all times. Our faith must be alive – a light of hope, a light in the midst of an indifferent world. It must be a light even in the midst of all the wonders of this world. We expect greater things than new technologies and inventions. We expect the overcoming of the powers of evil, of all the sin that still prevails. We expect the victory over all the misery that binds so many people, over all the evil and hostile powers that seek to torment us. This is our expectation. And this certainty will far surpass any apparent triumphs that the world flaunts through the work of its own hands.

In this expectation we will not become weary. In all our activities, we must live in Jesus Christ's future. Yes, there will always be some who complain, who want things to be different, who always think of the good old days and want to have them back. They are quite wrong, but they torment themselves and others as well. Away with the old! It is Christ's future we want!

The future of Jesus Christ must become a living reality in the experience of every Christian, in fact, for any-

one who longs for a different way. Your life must therefore be a piece of Jesus Christ's future, your life and
also your death. Our dying should not lead into death
but into life. Even in our last moments Christ's future
must touch us. The dying must exclaim, "The Savior is
coming!" Sinners, upon their awakening and repent-
ing, must confess, "The Savior is coming!" In this way
we will be watching. I know of no other way to do it.
In our own lives, right into the present, we have to experience his coming. This is the reality of Jesus Christ.

This watching is a part of our life, of our faith, of our
service to God. The Savior urges us seriously to "watch,
watch, watch!" as though he wanted to lay a foundation for it in our hearts, in our whole lives. It is as though
he were always waiting and asking, "How can I come
closer to this person, to that person? How can I meet
this one who is waiting for me? How can I go to meet
many at a time, so that again and again new victories
are given? What can I do to make the call, 'Jesus lives,
Jesus is victor!' heard throughout Christendom,
throughout the whole world?" For in our watching we
think not only of our own lives. We are watching for
the whole world. We are thinking of the world that is
still in darkness.

Do not fall, therefore, into the darkness of indifference, but watch! Your own hour will come – be prepared for it. Watch! Never lose heart. The Savior often

comes in the most difficult hour, in the most unhappy times. Watch, for the Savior is on the way! Watch for the world too. Do not give the world up as though it were lost for all eternity. It is true that the Savior's future brings separation. A judgment already lies in the fact that one person can come to faith while another remains outside for the time being. But this should not trouble us. The future of Jesus Christ is and will be a great and powerful help. All eyes will be opened (Phil. 2:9–11). Then people will weep and wail when they see how wrong they were; but their tears must contain the truth of Jesus Christ's future, of the Savior's coming, if the many are to receive help.

If only we could unite on this one point: to expect something from God.

We who have faith live in the future of Jesus Christ. Never shall we be able to say that the Savior has not come, that we have experienced nothing of Jesus Christ's future. This certainty is our joy; it is the wellspring of our Christian life. Let us remain in this joyful certainty every day of our lives. Let it fill our days, today and tomorrow. It will not abandon us. The fact that we are allowed to say, "The Savior is coming!" is like a surging tide of God's spirit. This tide will never end; it will continue to carry us forward, to lead us and strengthen us in all our thoughts and endeavors, in our whole life.

Therefore watch! Watch, all of you! Let each one be a fighter for Christ's future, a servant of the coming Savior. Give yourselves over to him, and let your hearts be prepared. Then Jesus Christ can come to you, into your house, into your hearts, into your lives. Never forget this: Watch! The Savior is coming!

No statement says
all that could be said.
No prayer fully
expresses our faith.

Oscar Romero

I am the Alpha and
the Omega, the beginning
and the ending, says the Lord,
who is, and who was, and
who is to come, the Almighty.

Revelation 1:8

5

Is God Still Dead?

A little while ago I was reading Nietzsche's *Thus Spoke Zarathustra*. Zarathustra had been staying in his cave in the mountains for years, reflecting about himself, and then he came out and wanted to leave that lonely place and go to the people again. And as he was coming down from the mountains, the first person he met was an old hermit. The hermit warned him not to go to the people and asked him what made him want to do a thing like that. "I love the people," Zarathustra told him. And the hermit said, "It was my love for people that ruined my life; that's what made me a hermit. I

love God now, not people." They finished their talk
and separated. And when Zarathustra was left alone
thinking about it, he was amazed, and said to himself,
"Who would have believed it! This good old man has
never heard – that God is dead!"

It made me shudder all over. And it's actually true –
God is dead! Of course he isn't really dead, but in the
lives of people he is dead. Nobody gets very excited if
you say "God"; that is one of the most boring things in
the world. When a rabbit jumps up in a field, everybody calls out, "A rabbit!" and shows a certain interest.
But for most people God is irrelevant. He is dead.

There is another way God is dead: our civilization
simply doesn't need God anymore. What good is God
when you are on the train? The man at the controls, it
is his job to get me to Stuttgart. The conductor can
groan, the fireman can break his back, the engineer can
worry, but isn't it all the same to me? I just sit there on
the train. That is why we can be so crude and ruthless
about enjoying everything these modern times offer us;
we do not need God. Science and technology do not
need God. They are succeeding quite well without him!
Hence the words, "They will look on him whom they
have pierced" – killed, that is. God is dead, murdered.
Nietzsche experienced more truth in his wrought-up
nerves than all the boring Christians, who don't have a
serious thought left for God! God is of no real impor-

tance, even for people with religion, because religion has become more important than God. Though people get into tremendous arguments about religious questions, all the time God is dead. And it is perfectly all right with them if he is dead, because then they can do what they like. That is another trait of our times, people want to be able to do whatever pops into their heads or feels good at the moment.

But that is just it: God in Christ is not dead, he still is the Alpha and the Omega. And everything in between is chaos, not just a spiritual alienation in which people don't know where life is going, but real chaos. Men and women are meant to share in the work for the end, for God's kingdom on earth, but they won't share. And so the madness goes on. This would be an eternal chaos except that Jesus came, and then a few followed him. But these few aren't the religious people, the ones that look out for their own salvation, those who just join in on religion for the good it will do them. No, Jesus' followers are people who put their lives at stake (Matt. 10:38). They are born of God, and they fight for God and for the earth. The church has no use for them, because the church wants to maintain itself as it is.

Nietzsche said, "God is dead," and he is right. But we say, "God is alive!" We don't want a good life, either in this one or in the other one. All we want is to know that God is alive. I don't want a minute of easy happiness

Nietzsche experienced more truth than all the boring Christians, who don't have a serious thought left for God.

Purely religious emotions – that's a measly business.

until this earth knows that God is alive! We must bow down under the living God and weep aloud for having killed him up to now. We are born for trouble, born for battle. Shame on us Christians who are always wanting to have it nice and soft, with a bit of God in our lives! We've got to fight until we're dead, or we aren't worth Christ's name. God calls out to us, "Share in my business!" and we are fooling ourselves unless we do this.

Abraham was told, "Come and take part," and there was no question. He did not ask, "Yes, but what will happen to me?" Anyone who asks that question is excluded and can't be a sharer. Only people who want to share in God's work, who want to get to the Omega and set the keystone in the creation, know the reality of God. The keystone is spirit, spirit in flesh and blood. We have to join this spirit again and again so that God's ending can come – the kingdom of God on earth.

This is what makes prophets; they don't fit into any Christian mold. Every prophet damns the Christians with their smooth and easy ways. The easy going is over and done with. When the prophets arrive they take drastic measures because they partake in God's interest.

Jesus is here on earth. You have to make a mental about-face, or you can't join in the work. Purely religious emotions, wanting to save our own skin – that's a measly business. You read what the prophets and apostles say. When did they ever think about saving their own skins? They went into death, into trouble and anxiety and suffering, into everything, because they were men who shared in the work with God (2 Cor. 4:7–12).

It hurts me to see so few who want to go into the fight. They come to me and pour out their worries. One wants me to pray for his headache, another for her soul, and both want little trouble, they want a salve so that nothing hurts. Nothing is meant to hurt anymore! But the chaos won't be beaten back without trouble and suffering and a fight to death. For the children of God there is nothing but fighting, nothing but standing firm and holding the standard for the rights of our God against everything that won't bow down under him (2 Cor. 10:1–6). And anything that doesn't come from God is of Satan – even if it happens to be a Peter who blocks the path of Jesus.

What we have to do now is to share God's work in the Spirit. Our little bit of Christianity won't save us from the terrible times when millions of people will be wiped out, unless God has people who share in the work for his kingdom. God's people are meant to do nothing else on earth but live and work and fight for the kingdom. "The kingdom is coming!" That was the way the disciples of Jesus Christ were. And this cry, "The kingdom is coming!" is actually the gospel. Unless there is an end to the earth's chaos, it is pure imagination to think that we have progressed or moved forward. Our civilization is a sham. We haven't made any real progress. Only when God's kingdom comes is there progress for mankind.

"'I am the beginning and the end,' says the Lord." Do we believe that? Believing is one thing, but getting down to living it out – that is something else. Let each one of us be earnest with himself and get off his soft bed. Even if it costs you your life, go right in, into the thick of the fight! Jesus is alive, and Jesus is victor, and he has given us our part to carry out.

But as we do our part, let us not forget that what finally matters is God's deeds, not ours. "With God we shall do valiantly!" (Ps. 108:13) This was said by David, who went to war without putting his trust in weapons. Sad to say, our faith does not bring about such deeds. The only kind of deed of God we know is something like founding an institution without the necessary money. If, after energetic begging, the money comes in, we call this a deed of God! This, and other things like it, are all that we know. These, however, are our deeds, not the deeds of God. They are all right, but we have to admit that they are but a makeshift solution until God comes and intervenes. To hope for deeds of the kingdom – that is faith. We must be beggars in the kingdom of God and not go away from the door until we have been given something from God. And we really need drastic deeds of God.

In this respect the game seems to be up today. God is simply not a reality for us anymore. Even in my own calling I scarcely ever bring about the living consciousness of God that I would really like people to have. True, I inspire many people, I give lofty thoughts to many people, but still something is missing, something that seems to have disappeared from our time. Human beings stand there, bleak and bare. The devout have lost their salt.

Believing is one thing, but getting down to living for God – that is something else.

The greatest deeds of God are not those that happen to sick people. These are not so important. It is much more important that we see things happening to the healthy, that we see changes in people's lives and in the state of the world. What kind of deed is from God? I would say, for example, it is when guns are no longer fired in war. Do you think this could be possible? Such a thought seems to make everybody chuckle! But did not deeds like this take place in Israel? (Josh. 5:13–6:27). Similar deeds are what we need today more than anything else so that everything is taken completely out of our hands and put into the hands of the living one. Of course, when something does come from God it will come at the right time and in God's way. What is necessary is that God's reality enters again into our lives.

This is what is lacking. God is not a reality for us. No other time has had so little of God. It is quite extraordinary. There is more religion than ever before, yet our hearts are much less filled with God. But we can be filled with such a joy that we can turn over a new leaf and so become genuine people, a changed people. To this end we want to be beggars. This will not come about through outward deeds but through something that happens from God and his kingdom. When this has been experienced, we have gained everything. Without it, God remains dead.

No confession brings perfection, no pastoral visit brings wholeness.

Oscar Romero

$\mathbf{J}$esus began to preach, "Repent,
for the kingdom of heaven is at hand."
So Jesus went throughout Galilee, teaching
in their synagogues, preaching the good
news of the kingdom…When he saw
the crowds, he began to teach them,
saying: "Blessed are the poor in spirit…
Blessed are those who mourn."

Matthew 4:17–5:16

6

The Kingdom
Is at Hand!

$\mathbf{I}$n the Sermon on the Mount, Jesus spoke about the
kingdom of heaven, and he was filled with a mighty
spirit, the spirit of the rule of God. It raised a storm
amongst his listeners when he said: "Repent! Become
quite a different person! Everything must change. The
kingdom of heaven is at hand!" That is, leave all your

preoccupations, give up all that has influenced you till now, and give up every power that has gripped you. A new kind of power is taking over. A new monarch is on the throne. A new king has assumed his reign. You shall have a new Lord over you. The old is passing away and a new time is coming.

It must have been a powerful spirit in Jesus that made the people shout, as with one voice, "What is that?" This spirit made them believe him and trust themselves to the Man from whom came the message for which many had been waiting: "That is he! That is the one through whom the almighty God is bringing in a new rulership, a new kingdom – that is he!" (John 6:14–15)

Although Christ spoke only of human matters, what he said was not at all acceptable to the earthly authorities. What he said was natural enough, yet it was much more. His teaching was not against human nature, but it did bring something of the divine into human affairs, something heavenly into the natural world. Indeed, it was as if earth would become paradise. People ate bread in the wilderness, where there had been none, and in place of sickness, health was given. Even those who had died were given new life. Joy came in all its fullness where there had been suffering and mourning.

All this took place in the most commonplace experiences of human life. No thrones were demolished, no special parties formed, no statues were erected –

everyone continued in his own house and his own place. But everyone, especially the poorest, had access now to something quite other, something from heaven, from God himself. When the kingdom of heaven comes close to us we experience something totally new. Into the life of each individual something amazingly alive comes. God's will is for life, for what is good, free, genuine, eternal.

God is not looking for heroic figures. He is looking for those who live from their hearts.

This is how the kingdom announces itself: the rulership of God is not visible through words alone, nor does it emerge from a different religious understanding, but it consists in deed and in truth (John 3:21). People become different because they are now living under a different rulership. This rulership is not a human government but the authority that comes from heaven into our hearts. And since it proclaims life, we are for life. Since this divine dominion rules by righteousness, we become righteous. In Jesus Christ, the Son sent by God, life on earth becomes fundamentally new. Such transformation does not come from your own efforts as you imagine. No, it comes through the strength and grace of God. The deeds of God come to us and a new world is built up through the strength and sheer joy in life: "The kingdom of heaven is at hand! Rise up and get going – away with all other dominion. Let God be your Lord!" This is what it means.

Is this still true for today? Sadly, almost two thousand years have passed and the world is still asleep. Instead of the reign of God, a Christian religion has been established. In the course of time it has become accepted that there is but one God, the Father; one Lord, Jesus Christ. Right up to this day, the Creator is recognized – and that is good. But the world is still sleeping under a canopy. Under this or that beautiful church roof every kind of dominion, other than God's, has crept in. Today we are subservient to many different authorities. Some of us are directed in one way, others in another, and each of us tend to "believe" accordingly. There are also religious empires: Catholic, Protestant, Lutheran, Methodist – in short, every possible denomination. But where is the reign of God?

There are also demonic empires: dominions of death; the rulership of avarice, which is rooted in money; and then all the need and poverty – yes the need – which drives people to greed and envy and fear. And so we stand again before the question: "Is the kingdom of heaven imminent?" Can we dare to say today, "Be on the watch, all of you! The kingdom is really on the way"? It has not come in nineteen hundred years; truly, it is proclaimed in the gospel, promised by God. But here we are again, subject to so many alien powers, all of them worthless compared with the rulership of God. Will it come one day?

"Yes! The kingdom will indeed come! Watch for it!" How dare I say this? Is it foolhardy of me to say this? No! I am completely certain of it, absolutely sure. Now is the time when we have to say, "Watch out, everyone! A new reign is about to begin." God's rule will dissolve all other authorities, even those we have so far taken to be good. But don't be afraid; the kingdom of heaven is coming! In today's decisive time, amid so much disharmony, dejection, commotion, where the urge is to put oneself first and in the center, to take the lead, to push agendas through, and for each party or group to be pitted against the other, each wanting to be in control – just in this day the kingdom of heaven is again drawing near. Today God wants to rule, and he is already making a beginning. Doubtless, in the time of Jesus it was a matter for derision when he said, "It is beginning today!" Today too, many people mock any proclamation that Jesus will establish his kingdom – but many also understand. Yes indeed, today is again a decisive hour! We must be equipped for the rulership of God, and this will not disgrace us.

We should love nothing more than to fulfill the justice of God, not in church services (which often attract people as honey attracts flies), but rather in our daily lives, wherever we are. That is when we have to work zealously for the commandments of God and his truth, yes, his rights; there we must show our hunger and thirst for righteousness; there we must prove whether or not we want God. We cannot prove that in our churches but must do it outside, in the fields, in business, in daily life, in your family – you husband, you wife, and you children. Together, we have to look out for the rights of God. You should be very fearful lest you neglect anything in the pursuit of righteousness – that is the condition.

True wisdom is found in the streets, not in palaces and lecture halls.

Therefore, "Repent, for the kingdom of heaven is at hand!" Be awake to the thought. Yes, today we must seize the opportunity for God's rulership. God's mighty hand can reach into our lives and we shall be different people – swept out of our old selves and living in a new time! We must gather together again. Who will come under God's rulership – who?

God is not looking for heroic figures – wonderful people – who captivate others with their charisma. It must have been quite baffling to the educated world when Jesus pronounced, "Blessed are the poor in spirit" – blessed are the uneducated, those who do not try to understand everything with their intellect! Blessed are they who do not have to impress others by showing how smart they are. Blessed are they who are not always theorizing about spiritual things. What Jesus is saying is that it is the day laborers who are blessed, those who live from hand to mouth and yet are skilled with their hoe or pickax. Blessed are the farm workers with their plow, who can't think much about anything except how best to do their work. Blessed are the craftsmen who create their handicraft and work hard to finish it on time but do not have time to read many books. Blessed are all such people whom we label uneducated – for these people are taught by God.

The kingdom of heaven belongs to such as these, those who are poor in spirit – for it is these who understand God, for they live according to their hearts. The others live according to their heads and thus cannot be used. They are too concerned about what might happen and don't leave the Father freedom to act. Therefore, those people are blessed who remain as children toward the Father in everything life brings them and do not set themselves up to be superior, as though the good fortune of the world lay in that. Praise God that true wisdom is to be found upon the streets and not in palaces and lecture halls (1 Cor. 1:18–25). God does not despise the humble, the insignificant, the poor. He sees the divine image in the simplest people; he sees the ardor of their hunger and thirst after righteousness. He sees the suffering of each one. He sees the broken ones who through their weakness have become humble, pure of heart, and merciful, and who do not make their hearts into a desert. He sees those who are sick with longing for the Savior's will. The Father sees the wearied workers, who are oppressed, working by the sweat of their brows. He sees everyone and accepts them all. To such as these the kingdom draws near.

How good it is that the rulership of God does not depend on the flaunted abilities of a few people who are at the top. No, his rulership first seeks out the sick, the poor, the abandoned. God's blessing is not a matter of improving the surroundings and decorating the houses of those who already have it made. This is why each person must become poor and remain so, so that it can never be said to anyone: "First you must acquire this or that, or else we can't make use of you!" In God's kingdom only one thing is required: a complete turnabout. If you are wealthy, let go of those ridiculous possessions! Say to yourself, "I will not let my money rule me. I won't envy those who have much. I want only the lordship of God!" If you are poor, turn completely away from your poverty. "I won't let cares and sorrows rule me. I want God to rule also in my greatest suffering. God will help me again. I will remain under his leadership."

So when you hear about God's kingdom, be true to it; that is the only thing required of us. Be faithful. Where alien influences creep in – away with them – we want God alone! Let nothing else have dominion; everything depends on this. Do not work yourselves up with worry. Your sinfulness, your worst qualities, your circumstance will be overcome when you become aware of how false the world is and how you have played along with it, and how the pure rule of God wants to break in. Then you can say: "Away with all else. Here the one pure Spirit rules!" Everything depends on that.

How good it is that the rulership of God does not depend on the flaunted abilities of a few!

Be faithful in your grief, in your hungering and thirsting for righteousness. Only be true to your Father in heaven (Matt. 5:38–48). Be merciful to those who persecute you, those who revile you. No swearword can hurt you. Let there be nothing else within your heart, in your suffering, in your poverty, in your affliction, or your care. Simply remain faithful to God's rulership and help others to do the same. Be compassionate toward others who are in need. Be meek with those who are malicious. If others try to pick a quarrel with you, make peace with them. Let nothing come from a false leading. Most of all, "Repent! Believe in the kingdom of heaven." We must prepare ourselves for this; be true to yourself, and be true to others. Then we can conquer the world, and all at once God's kingdom will come to us!

This kingdom – what does it consist of? In the first place, of comfort and suffering. When we are sinking in our need, which is still going on, however ghastly it is at the moment, this word of comfort penetrates and prevails: "God is indeed our Father and he will care for us!" That is the kingdom of heaven. That is also a great miracle. It cannot come about through words – there is no comfort for anyone in mere words! But the kingdom of heaven comes to comfort our sorrow. It comes to us sinners to bring us to righteousness. And it comes thus, so that the earthly kingdom also is brought into God's hand and into the hands of his people. It comes in mercy for the merciful, it brings peace to the peacemakers. It comes for the pure of heart so that they may see God as he is. All these are fragments of the kingdom of heaven. We may expect them today in faith.

In every misfortune, in each sin we commit, in all hunger and thirst, our longing is for the kingdom to break in. We believe in it, and we never want to lose it: "Father in heaven, we belong to you – we want to belong to nothing but your kingdom! It will be there for the poor, the burdened ones, the sinners, the sick, those who are oppressed, the poorest of the poor! It must be there for them, if only we believe and hold fast to it and never let it be taken from us. It must be visible today to everyone who believes in the name of Jesus the Christ!" Then the kingdom of heaven will come, and the deeds of the kingdom will be performed. Then it will be manifested to every heart; and finally it will also become visible throughout the world. Then it will manifest itself against the powers of darkness, against sin and death, against all violence and every false authority. This is how the kingdom of heaven will be established in every detail.

Those who cling to the past, who hold on to the wisdom of this world and to each human insight, are of no use. We must become whole, and we must never cease to entreat, "Father in heaven, we give ourselves up to you completely. We want to be your people." Who knows but that then this horrific need that has descended upon our earth might be averted? But if in our own cities there are so many who are so severely downtrodden, should we then just set up a howl and lament it? No, we must cry out, "Come, we want to help one another. We want to reach out to each one and relieve each special need. We want to join with you to become one people serving God. We want to take your hand and entreat God together that his kingdom shall dwell among us, that it shall become more established in our midst so that in actual deed and truth we can say, 'Here – here we have the deeds of God. Here we have not merely good people; here Jesus Christ is at work!'"

Thus we want to become salt, we want to be a light! We do not question that we are sinners; but God has called us, and we are determined to be ready. God must come to our help so that all other influences can be blotted out of our hearts, so that we shall become like the peacemakers, the merciful, the meek ones, standing true under God's rulership, throwing out everything that does not belong to it and rejoicing in adversity because of it. We shall thus come to know God's strength, God's majesty, God's consoling power, the first fruits of the heavenly kingdom. Then we shall become joyful that we have heard the call: "Repent, for the kingdom is at hand!"

No program accomplishes

the church's mission.

**Oscar
Romero**

Jesus sent two disciples, saying to them, "Go to the village ahead of you, and at once you will find a donkey tied there, with her colt by her. Untie them and bring them to me. If anyone says anything to you, tell him that the Lord needs them, and he will send them right away." The disciples went and did as Jesus had instructed them.

Matthew 21:1–6

7

Jesus Needs You – Not Your Religion

It is no good to prepare ourselves to receive God's coming by casting longing eyes to heaven, expecting something extraordinary to come from there and catch the attention of the whole world. It is only by actually standing up and fighting for the Lord that we can truly prepare ourselves for his coming. We are only prepared when we are determined, heart and soul here on earth, to becoming true disciples who, with the coming spirit of the Lord, want to set things right in accordance with God's truth and justice. We must not indulge in exalted spiritual feelings or in all kinds of speculations about the coming of Christ with the idea that this is the way to meet the Lord. It is better to think of how you can go to meet Christ now, on earth, and how you can be at his service with things as they are now.

This story shows how simple this can be: Two disciples are sent to fetch a donkey for Jesus to ride upon. They do this, and because they do it without thinking about it, they are servants in God's kingdom. After the owner of the donkey asks, "What are you doing? That donkey is mine," and they answer him, "Let us be, the Lord and Master has need of it," the owner does not stop to think about it, but out of respect to Jesus he surrenders the donkey to the Master. In so doing, he becomes a servant of God's kingdom because he does what is asked of him at the moment – the only true help to the Savior on earth.

We must write this deeply on our hearts. Consequently I say again, keep away from a lot of religious feelings. We must stand on the ground when the Savior comes and not float up into the air. Nowadays, unfortunately, many things are done with the idea that the more spiritual and otherworldly we are, the better. But it is just the other way round. The more we learn to seek truth and to act on it as far as possible in the situation in which God has placed us, even if that be in the dirt of the most perverted people and institutions, the better it is. For the Savior does not want to come as an idea but as a reality, wherever people live and struggle (Matt. 18:20). It is here that we must make way for him; and how can we do this except by acting in accordance with his nature and will? And his nature is simple, true, and genuine.

We must stand on the ground and not float into the air.

Every person who is waiting for Jesus can receive a distinct impression of what is right and good (Rom. 2:12–16). Perhaps he may feel that one or the other habit he has cannot be pleasing to God. If he stops it and changes, then he is making way for the one who comes. When our hearts are set on this practical kind of waiting, God will surely guide us every step of the way. In fact, all sincere followers of Jesus will be given so much practical work to do that – if you will permit me to say so – they will hardly have time for long devotions or for sitting in church (James 1:27).

It is the task of Jesus' disciples to put the nature of Jesus into action. This fact is generally not understood, since Jesus has been called a founder of a new religion. But that is not God's word to the world. His aim was never to give us a new religion in order that we might live a bit more decently – in that case Moses and his law would have sufficed.

The Savior is saying: "Don't make a religion out of me!"

With Jesus' simple command to the disciples the Savior is saying, "Don't make a religion out of me! That which I bring from God is not a religion, for all religions are rigid. They don't want to move forward, they don't intend to change. They set up shrines, they institute museums, they set up councils, and because of all this they are a stumbling block to the world." As a matter of fact – to be quite frank – our religions are a hindrance not only to the world but to the history of humanity.

Nothing is more dangerous to the advancement of God's kingdom than religion: for it is what makes us heathens. But this is what Christianity has become. Do you not know that it is possible to kill Christ with such Christianity! After all, what is more important – Christianity or Christ? And I'll say even more: we can kill Christ with the Bible! Which is greater: the Bible or Christ? Yes, we can even kill Christ with our prayer. When we approach God with our prayers full of self-love and self-satisfaction, when the aim of our prayers is to make our world great, our prayers are in vain.

The Savior will not allow himself to become petrified in religion. That is why the Savior told the story of the ten virgins, some of whom were wise and others not (Matt. 25:1–13). With this, he says, "There are some who make a religion out of me, a cozy haven, a state of bliss. It is the others who will be the living Christians, always open to change, always seeking something new, until the entire world stands there renewed." So ask yourselves: are you ready to go for it, or aren't you?

Dear friends, we must grasp how important it is to surrender ourselves completely. There is so much Christianity in which hearts are not subjugated, so much religiosity that leaves people just as they were before. The way to serve Jesus, to go to meet God, has not yet been understood. People think they do this with churches, sermons, and worship meetings, but it is not done in this way. This way of doing things has become so rooted in us that it costs a tremendous effort to turn around and find again what will really prepare the way for the kingdom of God.

When Jesus speaks it is always a social matter, a matter for humanity. What Jesus did was to found the cause of God on earth, in order to establish a new society that finally is to include all nations – in contrast to the societies we have made, societies where not even true families can be formed; where fathers do not know how to care for their children; where friendships are formed and torn apart; in short, where everyone lives in heartache. Faced with this wretched social order, Jesus wants to build a new one. His word to us is this: "You belong to God and not to these man-made societies."

Nothing is more dangerous than religion: it is what makes us heathens.

Recently I read a little book by a Russian clergyman in which he says that we need neither churches nor cathedrals – a barn will do just as well. This, however, is beside the point. Jesus is not the founder of a new religion; he renews life. We must love the word of God spoken to humankind; and if we are to love it, we must first understand that this word is much greater than the Bible. It cannot be chained, written down as if set in cement. When God's word is frozen, even the best Christians are able to justify their hate toward their fellowmen, even killing them and vehemently separating themselves from them. No! God's word is a word that binds, and yet it is a word of freedom.

As free people, your only loyalty is to God, and your duty is to work so that God enters into this miserable, lost, cursed society. Now compare this word of God with our Christianity. Today there are Christians who believe that they will (after death or at Jesus' return) fly with the Savior to heaven and then laugh at those left behind. I find it incomprehensible that those who call themselves devout consider themselves better than others or exempt from God's judgment. This kind of religion is false because it separates me from other human beings. I will have nothing to do with that! Jesus entered right into the human condition in all its ugliness. He united with people. He did not separate himself from us. In the same way I want to come alongside the lowest people in hell and not separate myself. I want to see who is finally deemed righteous, and whether Jesus is not greater than our righteousness.

Do not be offended, then, if I say that people today think of the kingdom of God as much too supernatural and as something completely foreign to our human condition. They think that some day something will come down from heaven that will change everything all at once as if by magic, and that in the meantime it is all right to let life go on as it is, so long as we attend to our religious duties. Things have gone so far that you can meet extremely religious people living in horribly untrue and unjust circumstances, and they don't even lift a finger to change anything. Their faith might one day have to be called a fraud. You know well that to such the Savior comes like a thief (1 Thess. 5:1–2). Yet the Savior also comes like a conqueror.

Therefore, if we would put right what we can in ourselves because Jesus lives in us, and if we would work only for the good, then the way for him would be properly prepared. Even if much remains that, in the end, only he can put right, we will show that we are people who are not simply waiting for their salvation in a self-centered, self-loving way, but who rather are consumed by eagerness to smooth the way for God, even if it is only in a very small way.

Yes, everything – I tell you everything – that is and comes from God's kingdom must first be prepared on earth. This must become more and more practical so that in the end it can be tangibly grasped. We must make an effort for him where we live, where we work, so that in all we do we do it for the sake of God. Then we won't have to concern ourselves about whether the Savior will return tomorrow or in a thousand years. We will already live for his coming. The kingdom of God becomes our cause and is revealed to us in life more and more clearly and surely, because with this attitude we are able to experience something from God.

So let everyone consider: How can I show obedience in some way, out of love to Jesus the Lord? Yes, *today* how can I show obedience? There is always great joy in heaven whenever someone does something for God. It can be quite a small thing, but it shows whenever one thinks only of being obedient, obedient to any true word that strikes the heart. All heaven is eager for such disciples. We have enough people who pray, who attend meetings and services. And more than enough people who argue about what they believe to be right or wrong. But of doers, heaven has not enough! There are not enough people who grasp that in the first place it is not knowledge, or doctrine, or preaching, that is lacking. What is lacking is right living, and this will only come about when people together take up a more truthful and genuine attitude for the sake of God.

This must be our attitude. An enthusiasm must burn in us, not merely to pick up some spiritual refreshment, but to do something for Christ, something that is right and true before him and his authority. Let us go at it enthusiastically, dear friends. This is the way we will go to meet God's kingdom. Oh, if I could only make that clear to all who read this! So much depends upon the disciples of Jesus being inwardly so disposed that a rich spring of living, of active life, flows from them through which their whole being, always under control, can flourish until the moment when they can belong wholly and completely to the Lord.

Christianity can kill Christ. So can the Bible.

Unfortunately this matter of being disciples is a difficult thing, which is why Jesus had so few of them (Matt. 7:21–27). Anyone who cannot follow a command, a word that comes to him in truth, will not find the kingdom. You will not come into the kingdom unless you obey! The most harmful thing to the kingdom of God is that so few want to be obedient. Instead, everyone cultivates his own special brand of spirituality. There are now a thousand expressions of spirituality: in short, every kind of piousness. But where is the person who will obey God's simple command when it comes to him in truth and submit to it?

Where is the person who will allow himself to be thrown into the gutter for God and Jesus and yet remain true, like Peter? Such a person knows in his heart, "Jesus is the way! I will follow him for death or life! Even though this goes against all my thoughts and feelings, Jesus is victor! I will stay with him."

I tell you, Jesus will come as a conqueror and will strike you down without mercy unless you are obedient people, in spite of all your hopes for God's kingdom (Rev. 3:1–3). Even if you are weak, it doesn't matter as long as you can say, "I will follow! I will follow! I will follow! Wherever I see truth, I will go straight to it and not pause to consider. I will serve Jesus for the sake of God!" Only in this way will there be a circle of disciples around Jesus upon whom he can depend. He doesn't need strong people, nor so-called confident, bold, trained, or courageous people who push things ahead in the world. He needs people who are broken, who fear lest they become disobedient to his command. Those are the people he needs, for they are servants. All the others who have a manufactured piety and feel themselves so secure in it, are for the most part hardly usable as servants. But those who fear and tremble, those who are shaken and shocked by the word of truth yet joyfully say yes and take action – these are his people.

Therefore we must learn to surrender ourselves in a very simple, practical way, and go at it with zeal: "I will surrender myself; I will keep God's cause uppermost in my heart so that it may come to be on earth." We want to live in such a way that here on this earthly plane something visible may happen that will bring honor to God.

May God grant that we grasp this and are confident in it. It is so easy and simple and clear that any child can understand it. Let everyone, in his own place, become obedient. Listen! Listen, children, when something that is right is said to you, and be eager to do it. You, young men and young women, if you know that something is right, do it! You older ones, men and women, if you see that something is right, do it! And anyone else among us, sick or healthy, high or low, impoverished or not – if you know that something is right, then do it! Don't think too long about it. Just consider: is it right, or not? If it is right, go at it. Then you will find Christ.

No set of goals
and objectives
includes everything.

Oscar Romero

What shall we say then? Shall we go on sinning so that grace may increase? By no means! We died to sin; how can we live in it any longer?… The death Jesus died, he died to sin once for all; but the life he lives, he lives to God. In the same way, count yourselves dead to sin but alive to God in Christ Jesus.

Romans 6:1–11

8

The New Life

The apostle Paul writes about a new condition of life. This idea is foreign to us now. What do we know of death? We are always trying to preserve our life, fretting over earthly things and filling our hearts with the desires of this life – this same life that already contains the worms that are a sign of our corruption. And yet things should have changed by now with us

Christians in that we should reign as kings in life, and death should no longer dominate everything. The Lord Jesus brings this about. He has made it possible for a new condition of life to begin in us.

Previously, as the apostle says elsewhere, death became king through Adam's sin to the damnation of all (Rom. 5:12). They died and could not be helped. No help existed. The Lord could temporarily protect and shelter a few through the promise, but in reality all people were subject to the law of death. Death was king and the only power on earth. But now, through Christ, a new life has come into being. Because of his deed, life will now rule. Now by a word of justice everyone shall be released from damnation to enter into life. Our whole being will be immersed in this, and we ourselves shall rule over life (Rom. 8:1–2).

At first sight it looks as though Jesus has done everything, arranged everything. Now everybody may receive grace and be able to live in God's grace. Shall we go on sinning now, since everything is so easy and Christ has done everything for us? Can we sit back and relax, thinking, "God be praised and thanked, the Savior is very loving, he saves me. He saves me! Of course, I am still a terrible sinner, but the Savior saves me through grace!" So people lie around and live like everybody else, without thinking that Christ's righteousness should cause us to set things right. We must go into the new condition of life with our whole being – not just skim around it, comforting ourselves that everything is now all right, that Jesus has made everything right and will prepare everything for us. No! We must move into the newness of life with our whole being and really have living soil under our feet. There is no other way if we understand the Savior rightly, and that is what baptism means. Baptism is nothing less than an event that allows us to partake of Christ's death so that we may live with him and enter into the new life. Baptism is there for us to die to sin and to be buried in the flesh with Christ so that we too may enter into the resurrection of Jesus. Just as he was awakened from the dead by the glory of the Father, so we too are to begin a new life.

Everybody wants to be saved, but who has any real desire for a new life?

Thus the death of Jesus Christ, or the dying to our selfish nature, is transmitted to us by the Savior by means of baptism. This should grip us so that our whole being responds with a yes. I no longer have to worry about this life of sin. I can strive for something different! "Therefore, if anyone is in Christ, he is a new creation; the old has gone, the new has come!" (2 Cor. 5:17)

We must become filled with zeal, with joy and gratitude, gladly enduring anything, however hard, in order to be free of death and of this life in the midst of death. Then the powers of the resurrection come closer to us; then Christ really becomes the risen one, and a new life comes into being. Not the kind of life we have been

Today's Christian cultivates a sofa lifestyle.

seeking until now, trying to be a little better than other people, thinking that it is a new life if we steal a little less or walk around a little more decently than before or wear a more respectable coat, or if we exchange a criminal's cap for something more acceptable. All this is supposed to be a new life? Bah! It is not at all a question of being better than you were before. The new life means that forces for life can now be seen within you, that something of God and of heaven, something holy, can grow in you. It means we can actually see that it is no longer the sinful desires that have power, but that there is something of Christ's resurrection, something of his life that has power through the Spirit and that leads you toward wholeness.

Oh, how far most of us Christians are from this! How I bemoan the fact that it is all so far away from us. Oh, that our lives might be revealed to us and that we might see how the old life still clings to us. Then we might experience wholehearted desire for what is new. Everybody wants to be saved, but who has any real desire for a new life? Are we not a long way from risking our own skins? Each of us has a certain layer of skin around us, and we want to stick to that skin and go to heaven in it. For most people it is too scary to think of giving up their own selves. They feel so very comfortable in that old skin and will not surrender it at any price. Recently I spoke to someone who is highly regarded in Christian circles. He has set himself up very nicely and comfortably in a splendid house where everything is just wonderful. At the same time he is supposed to be a pastor and to preach, which he does. But when I saw him there amid all his comfort, I said, "Listen! You are rotting away under all this!" But people would rather lie down on their sofa, and on the most comfortable one to boot! They just do not see how this leads to death (Matt. 19:16–23). Yes, along with our Christianity, today's Christian now cultivates his sofa lifestyle, his religious knowledge and conduct and all the rest of it, believing that now he has attained the very best that Christ has to offer.

Oh, dear people! Let us each ask ourself whether we do not have a little corner somewhere that we like to crawl into and not be pulled away from. There we lie; and God can knock and preach as much as he likes, but we will not come out. This is why the church as a whole does not come to a new life in which something of God is revealed. Many people take it to mean something a little better than their old life, something more moral – but that is not what Christ came to bring! What is meant is a life in which something of God really can work and which shows that God lives and Christ lives, a life in which spiritual things are no longer idle talk but a reality. What stupid people Christians often are! Most Christians have absolutely nothing worth saying

simply because they have so little to show. The new life
that Christ came to bring never quite reaches into
the temporal and earthly things, never overcomes this
world.

We must make a completely new beginning. I keep
coming back to this same point. We need to begin completely anew again and again, more deeply, more thor-
oughly, more fully. We must do this until we really have
laid a new foundation for which to have a Savior. For if
we really reach a point where we are united with Christ
in a death like his, we shall certainly be united with
him in a resurrection like his. Then we will enter into a
completely new life. What a tremendous thing it is to
meet the resurrection!

The apostle Paul was well aware of what the new life
meant, and therefore all his letters ardently declare that
we should no longer serve our sinful nature, our flesh.
All self-serving must be left behind. Thus Paul writes,
"For His sake I have suffered the loss of all things and
count them as refuse, in order that I may gain Christ"
(Phil. 3:8). Individuals like Paul have experienced
something of God, have heard something, touched something, absorbed something. God is no longer a theory or
an idea: "That which we have seen with our eyes and
touched with our hands, concerning the word of life, we
testify to. This is the message we have heard from him
and proclaim to you, that God is light and in him is no

darkness at all" (1 John 1:5). We want to have nothing more to do with darkness! Away with it all!

Then the new world comes to meet us, something new comes in, and it goes without saying that the sinful life will cease. This does not mean that we simply say goodbye to this world, for even if we chase our sinful personality out the front door, the next minute it will come in again by the back door. No matter how we chase it, we cannot get rid of it – unfortunately! We can only sigh over it. But we must sigh in all earnestness, not with the thought at the back of our minds that we get to keep this or that part of our nature and somehow squeak through when the Savior comes. No, we should sigh as though we really want to participate in divine things and want to be those who receive something of God, of the resurrection of Christ. We should be as zealous for this as we are for success in jobs. For men and women really become zealous in their careers, working all day and during the night to make sure they do not lose anything! That is how zealous we should be. That is what we should do for the kingdom of God. It should be part of our flesh and blood to be fighters for God's kingdom, fighters for the new world. Otherwise God's benefit will in the end also escape us.

I am afraid for us. Though I have preached a great deal, my general impression is always the same. In a few individuals a little is at work, but it is quite remark-

Most Christians have nothing worth saying simply because they have so little to show.

able what resilience people have. It is exactly like a little rubber band that one pulls up high. When one lets go, it snaps right back; the old self is there again. We are the same afterwards as we were before. Are we really concerned about whether or not we will be able to come through? When things become more serious, when everything is on the line, will we have enough energy to want to belong to the Savior? Or will we love our own lives more than him? You do not need to worry that the Lord Jesus will forsake you. Only take care that you do not forsake him. See that you are not taken by surprise like Lot's wife and that your possessions are not more important to you than the Savior. When he comes, many will be so surprised. Instead of bowing before him they will first of all jump to their wallets or into their kitchens. The freedom of Christ will not be discernible in them.

Now, do you not feel Paul's zeal? He also was worried, which is why he wrote his letter to the Romans. And why did he write to them in this way? He was afraid they were dragging Christianity into the dirt and that they felt they had nothing more to do – the Savior had died and risen again, and that was that! The apostle is dismayed and thus exclaims, "Do you want to remain like this? Do you want to end up in the flesh, having begun in the Spirit? The Savior cannot help you unless you have turned to something quite new" (Gal. 3:3). But if we have died with Christ and are like him, then we shall also live with him. Now he lives, and once we have broken through the whole worldly structure – completely, not halfway – the new world can shine upon us; and only then will we have nothing more to do. Then we shall no longer live for sin but for God, as Christ now lives for God.

To live freely for God. Oh, if only this were so! To live no longer for our castles, no longer for our wealth, none of this, but to live for God alone. Oh, if only this would happen! May the Lord have mercy on us! May he soon open up the heavens so that we can understand, for it almost seems that people just do not understand and that all is in vain. But let us not lose courage. A new time is coming. Even if only a few desire earnestly and zealously to strive toward God with their lives, it is coming. And in death they will find life.

This is what we are about:

We plant the seeds

that one day will grow.

Oscar Romero

May I never boast except in the cross of our Lord Jesus Christ, through which the world has been crucified to me, and I to the world. Neither circumcision nor uncircumcision means anything: what counts is a new creation. Peace and mercy to all who follow this rule, even to the Israel of God.

Galatians 6:14–16

9

Forget Yourself for God

The Lord of Creation, the God of the nations, has other people than us. We Christians are not exactly the most important and best in the world! We are only one group, but there are also others (John 10:16). It is very kind of God to include us among them. We should not only think of this more often, we should feel it. We need to pull ourselves together, for God's sake much more than for our own. That is why I cannot tolerate this incessant wanting to be saved. I am so angry about our church because it only instructs people how to be saved. We should first long to be set right.

Just like a scoundrel of a son who makes demands and wants to be made happy, so there are Christians who seem to always want to be the first and foremost. They laugh the angels to scorn. They are the proudest people in the world, never thinking what unclean company they would make in heaven. We should think about this more. If we are children of God, then being saved is ultimately a secondary matter. The main thing is to work, to work out our salvation (Phil. 2:12–13). All our thoughts and desires should be aimed toward seeing that not we but God is glorified among all people. It is not a question of our looking forward to dying and going to heaven. No! If I am a child of God, the first thing to learn is to forget myself and seek a new creation. This is so misunderstood.

If we seek first our salvation and then the kingdom of God, there will never be any light on the earth. Misery will increase and the darkness will not be held back. There may well be many who rejoice in the blessedness of heaven, but on earth, misery and need will increase with each passing year. God has therefore given us a new motivation, moving our hearts to cry out, "No! We will not think first of our salvation. We will not seek our own good first! We want to be servants! We want to seek God's salvation, God's glory, God's kingdom!"

We do not first want to save ourselves and be satisfied with this. But we want to take to heart the sighing of all creation, the lamenting and groaning of countless human beings who are certainly not helped by our salvation, but are only helped if we cry out and pray: "Thy kingdom come!" They are helped only when we experience God's intervention with heated fighting and struggling and with the surrender of our own well-being, even of our own salvation.

To this the church is called, and because of this I cry out, "Forget what is yours! Deny yourselves. Go with Jesus to the cross for the glory of God, and leave your salvation to the creator of all things (Luke 9:23–27). Do not think of yourselves; think of the grieving heart of your Father, who longs to have his peace come to every creature." But who is there to help him? Who will sacrifice himself and take up the cross? Who will give up his own pursuits, as good as they may be, in order to serve the Father? Which of us, especially us Christians, will give up the happiness of this world? Who will permit God's judgment upon him, who will seek the hand of God to carry out justice on the earth?

The church only instructs people how to be saved. We should first long to be set right.

The Bible tells of the fight in which the early Christians found themselves and what a terribly hard time they had. Out of a thousand Christians today, however, scarcely one would be able to endure such a struggle. The first Christians were looked upon as outcasts, very much as gypsies are looked upon in our day. They were viewed as not belonging to the educated class, for they had only a "crucified one" as God. What foolishness to have such a God! (1 Cor. 1:26–31) In our time we have no concept of what this really means. Today it is easy to believe in the crucified one and to be a Christian – but in those days one was thought to be a complete fool. This is why the apostles used so many lofty expressions concerning our salvation. They sought to strengthen the church, which found itself in the heat of battle, in order that it might not tire in the fight but would instead keep the prize, the precious jewel, before its eyes. That is Paul's main purpose in talking about salvation.

Today we cry, "Oh, to be saved!" But God says, "I do not need you in heaven; I have enough saved ones here. I need workers, people who get things done on earth. First serve me there."

I wish with all my strength that all this religious warmth and comfort, which keeps Christians always looking to heaven instead of living rightly on earth, would die. Today's Christians are so deceived in their warm feelings of salvation. What nonsense! If you do not want to become dust for God, if you do not think of his name rather than your own, then, if your hearts are tormented, you have no sympathy from me. Anything done that is not done for God is in vain. If you believe in Jesus, but only in the sense of what you will gain, you will never overcome the world.

Our salvation is meant for only one purpose: to honor the Father. When we honor the Father we do so in the way he manifests himself on earth. We lay aside our own glory, even if this contradicts the way we feel and think. Away with it! We seek the truth and justice of the Lord in the Savior. We can only ask, "Is it true, or is it not?" Everything depends on our finding truth and justice and upon righteousness being revealed on earth. Everyone, in his own place or position, can join in with this. It does not depend upon a system of belief. If a person is sincere and wants Jesus in truth and justice, then he will be welcome.

We must take seriously what Jesus desires to be on earth! If there are no people in whom Jesus can live, if religious people live their lives mindlessly, if we Christians let all the scriptural passages and prayers roll off our tongues as thoughtlessly as a parrot sounds off, and if we simply relate them to our precious little selves without stopping to consider whether the conditions of our life and of our world are right – then it is our fault if nothing new breaks into our lives. On earth this principle prevails: if you do not want to submit yourself completely, surrender yourself entirely, then God will look for someone else.

Do you want to have "religion," to wheedle your way out of everything and say, "God does all things for us! Oh, how I am looking forward to heaven; how nice it will be there"? If this is what you want then you will be surprised to hear, "What are you and your piety doing here? You should have been faithful on earth. You should have given up everything so that Jesus might live here among us." Where shall God be revealed? On earth. Not in heaven. He does not need you there where there are already plenty of angels to honor him. Your place is on earth! This is the salvation the angels long to observe (1 Pet. 1:10–12).

Take it seriously. Our deeds and life, our redemption, belong to the earth. "Your kingdom come, your will be done on earth as it is in heaven." This is not the hopeless place that people think it is. Much can be done on this earth. What counts is a new creation. Christ's future belongs to it! More can happen here for God than if a hundred thousand people die "saved." But who can understand this? Only those who allow *Jesus* to be glorified can understand it – those who give themselves to death so that Jesus lives.

If, however, we as Christians do not judge ourselves, the world will remain the same no matter how much we achieve materially, building railroads and installing telephones throughout Africa, or in one day sending out thousands of missionaries to the lost. By this we may indeed change some ideas or make some improvements of an earthly nature, but the situation will remain the same. We humans can accomplish nothing. We may attend to this and take care of that, but actually we should only look toward what Jesus does and will do. Our only concern should be that he, the coming one, lives; that he, the victor and ruler, lives in us. Then, through him, we may perhaps be used. Then, through him, our salvation may count.

"I don't need you in heaven," God says. "I need people who get things done on earth."

If we view things in this way, we shall receive a name and be known as people who can be used. But we must be used on God's terms, not ours. So many people want to spread "Christianity" and "Christian culture" among the unbelieving, but it is really a serious question whether the lost receive the glory of God when they receive us. The evangelicals say, "If only everybody were saved, God's name would be glorified." The churchly people say, "If only everybody would go to church, then the name of the Lord would be glorified." I don't believe it! That is not how he will be glorified. Such means do not glorify God unless a divine power comes into people's lives and changes their situation.

We can preach as much as we like, but people keep on going to church for their own sakes – not for God's. Just test it out: if you preach something they don't like, they grumble. If it is something they like, they praise it. If they don't get something out of it for themselves, then they think it is false, or they go elsewhere. Today so many people go to church but so few are really changed. A few may be, but in too many cases church-goers persist in their sinful, worldly ways. Nothing truly changes.

It should be unbearable to those of us who believe if we are worthless for the task for which we have been put on earth (Eph. 4:1). We have been placed in the midst of creation, but sadly we have lost the feeling that we are here for a purpose, not for ourselves, but for something far greater – to be servants of the living one. This is what makes us feel so sad, so defeated. People mostly sit in church thinking only about themselves. Each one bemoans his own lot and looks for something in himself and for himself, without really knowing what God's purpose for the earth is. One would like to cry out to them all, "Good people, forget yourselves! Think of God's cause! Start working for that! Or at least be sorry, not that things are going badly for you, but that you have nothing better to do than concern yourselves with your own petty affairs."

The most terrible thing for us is that God cannot really use us. No wonder that we degenerate despite our advancements. Every one of us will degenerate, even in temporal things, if we are not active as part of a greater whole with higher goals. But anyone who works with love and joy for something greater than himself will thrive, even in the worst of earthly circumstances. All the values of life, both physical and spiritual, will be destroyed if we do not, as human beings, have work to do for the life of the earth, for creation, for God.

I wish I could hammer this into your hearts, dear friends. Much more could come if we would forget ourselves and think of that higher, more important cause for which we are here. And Jesus will help us in this. He is the brightness and radiance of God on earth (Heb. 1:3). God continues to shine in this Man, for Christ is there for God's purpose, not ours. That is his significance, that is why he has eternal life, even if nailed to the cross. He is there for a purpose – God's purpose. As for us? It seems as if any fly can destroy us because we drift along with no purpose outside of ourselves. But with Jesus it is different. The Father of the creation shines through him. And because this Man knows what it is to serve, creation feels a renewed hope that everything will be brought to order again and that the ruined earth, which has become a wilderness, will be restored again for God.

This is why the Savior came. And for this reason he will come again. To be sure, Jesus is personally and closely bound to each person, but if we do not want to help him, if we do not want to prepare the way, then he must set us aside. Lest you forget, the Savior is there for God, and only after that for you. "My food," Jesus said, "is to do the will of him who sent me and to finish his work" (John 4:34). We Christians have turned this completely around, believing that Jesus came only for us. We flatter ourselves in this way with the illusion of having Jesus for our own. But I tell you, the Lord will not care about us if we do not want to help him. He can put us all aside, for he works for God and not for us. Therefore, do not flatter yourselves anymore. He has already begun to cut the threads, and who knows how it will all work itself out?

Over the centuries people have only thought about how they could profit most from the Savior. But there will soon be little profit left in our pockets if the thought does not also come, now I want to serve! Now I want to be something for God! I will not be concerned about myself any longer (Mark 10:45).

That is why the sense of peace and grace escapes so many Christians. The profit and power of grace is soon used up if we are here with no purpose, if we do not see that we are what we are for God's sake. If we do not learn to understand our relationship to the earth as one in which we are called to work upon it for God and his kingdom, our lives will dissipate in utter aimlessness.

Christians today are just like the world. At bottom there is no difference. The attitude of Christians toward what is worth living for is not one whit different than that of the unbeliever. True, we know more about God and about Jesus, but we are covetous and have kept everything for ourselves, not only spiritual things but material things too, much more so than all the unbelievers. And so, with all our knowledge, we are in the end worse than the most ignorant of non-Christians. Can't you see this?

Today is a time when God casts his eyes upon the earth to see who can be used. Used, that is, without distinction. Whatever clothes you may wear on earth matters nothing to heaven. It is not a question of who you are, to whom you belong, the thoughts you have grasped or what creed you hold to. The question is whether your heart is open for the coming glory and radiance of God upon earth. Then it does not matter what or who you are. I think that today the Muslims, the Jews, just as much as all the different kinds of Christians – of which there are an embarrassingly wide range – are all being looked at by God to see whether they have lives that can stand unafraid before God at

Lest we forget, the Savior is there for God, and only after that for you.

his coming. If that is the case, then the time can quickly come for them to be called. Perhaps for now they do not know very much about heavenly matters. But if their heart is right, they can still be used (Ps. 51:17).

And so a time of humanity is approaching, yes, a time of humanity when God will be glorified in his people. If you think a time of Christianity is coming, the Christianity we see around us today, then you are mistaken. A time of humanity is coming, for Jesus is the glory of humankind in heaven, and God is no respecter of persons. Whoever fears God and does right is pleasing to him. Outward differences play no part.

Does this depress you? Are you sad? Do you say, "But I have been a believer for so long and now non-Christians are to be placed on an equal footing with me!" Is that what you say? Why? You see in the Savior only an advantage for yourselves! Then it will be with you as it was with Jonah.

But believe me, you Jews, you Catholics, you evangelicals, you Muslims, believe me – all of you. Today God's only concern is whether you want to be of any use to him. Do you want him to be glorified in you or not? Just say yes. No gentile will be excluded. Just say yes, and everything else will be given too. This should be a day when thousands and thousands pledge themselves only to God: "We want to be your people once more. We want to belong to you again on earth. How shamefully has creation been defiled! How shamefully have the nations dishonored your name! How shamefully have we dealt with everything on earth, following the lusts and greed of our hearts! But now our eyes are opening. The life of the world is being dissipated at our hands. And we will ruin it completely if we do not fulfill your purposes for it. Therefore we pledge to you, almighty God, that we want to be here only for you, with all our heart and soul. Whatever happens to us, we want to sacrifice our bodies and our lives, everything, so that once again there may people who prepare the way with all their heart."

Those who will not forget themselves and surrender their lives to God and become something for him on earth will have no part in the Savior. However pious they may appear to be, it will all be to no avail. The severest times of God are coming over the earth, for the sighing of creation has ascended to him. If we continue standing in God's way, we will be nothing in his sight anymore. Therefore I ask you – make a start! The others will soon follow. Vow to God that you want to serve him, however poor and insignificant you may be. Forget yourselves. Have pity for your King. Have compassion for your God who has been so miserably cheated by us mortals.

And even if you cannot translate this right away into an outward, visible deed, nevertheless a grieving and crying out for God should stir your hearts even now. We must humble ourselves and feel deeply distressed that we have served our God on earth so little. Then the Savior will come. Then something in us will change, renewing our whole person and making us fit to glorify God in a new life for his kingdom.

We water seeds
already planted,
knowing that they hold
future promise.

**Oscar
Romero**

> See, I lay a stone in Zion,
> a tested stone, a precious corner-
> stone for a sure foundation;
> the one who trusts
> will never be dismayed.
>
> Isaiah 28:16

10

God Is Seeking a Zion

Whenever God's cause on earth is about to leap forward, God always creates a Zion. That means a community of people who live a distinct life and keep an open heart and mind for God's working and speaking. There has never been any illumination from God given to the world without such a reality. Laws that are right in themselves become living and true only in connection with such a Zion. Without a Zion we wither and die away. Thus many doctrines produce something relatively good only as long as they are alive in hearts that seek God and form a Zion. But if this Zion ceases,

113

even the best of dogmas will die off, and the church that they have made for many to dwell in will totter.

This is not always to be regretted, because anything that has come into being within time is only relatively good, and whenever divine truth comes to expression in words and institutions it is bound to reflect the imperfection of our human condition. Repeatedly, it has to give way to something more perfect, until the perfection of God's kingdom can make its full appearance (1 Cor. 13:9). Thus our confessions of faith, our denominations, show signs of not remaining firm. Numerous people are withdrawing from them openly or unobtrusively, and however much we may want to help God's kingdom by binding them anew to confessions and creeds, we shall not succeed. Noble-minded, God-seeking people can no longer subscribe to them. We should therefore never suppose that those who withdraw from church and creed do so because they want to have nothing to do with God. On the contrary, there are many who do not want to forsake God but seek him, and so they strive after something different from that which has appeared so far.

That can be a consolation when we are approaching a time in which we are experiencing great changes. A movement may yet come into being, one that at first may walk in doubt and unclarity, but nevertheless provides the soil from which a new shoot springs up that proves to be a Zion of God, for whose sake God can call into life new ideals founded on eternal truth. To be sure, we must be very careful not to accept anything too quickly. Great zeal for our religious persuasions can be very disastrous and possibly become directly opposed to God. Let us remind ourselves that Jesus himself opposed this, and those who were zealous for an existing structure of God's people became in time enemies of God's will (Luke 11:52–53). It can also be like that now. The great devotion that so many people spend upon various church organizations and ministries, each of which holds itself to be necessary, is proof enough of how much of the human spirit there is in today's religion. What is human is imperfect and cannot be preserved forever. So let our works collapse, and those of God will break forth all the more clearly.

Never judge those who withdraw from church and creed. They are often the very ones who seek after God.

However, we should not wait in a merely fatalistic way for something new and better, but instead surrender ourselves for it. I repeat, if something from God is to break forth in the world, there has to be a Zion – a community under his rulership. Without that it will not happen. Already with Abraham and his servants, along with his son, there had to be a united fellowship of souls wholly directed toward God, souls able to renounce themselves and all they owned in order to be prepared for God to act. Even these people were then God's Zion. God has always sought out such people, right up to the present.

It is the same with Moses as with Abraham. With Moses a foundation stone and corner stone was laid in Zion. Now the events of Zion could begin. God's spirit swept, as it were, out of Zion and overcame the world. But Zion was nothing more than a few people who sacrificed themselves completely for it. That is how it was again and again in Israel. If this people of Zion was missing, the rulership of God was missing. Again, Samuel had to be a man of Zion, and to the extent that he was so, the rulership of God was present. At times when the nation fell away from God, David and the prophets had to be the people who lived for God alone, in order to draw others to themselves for God's purpose, in self-denial and sacrifice of their whole being.

Later, when Israel was languishing in captivity, God could not simply help. Certainly the people's hearts were in need of help, but they were unable to surrender themselves to receive it. How can God help under these circumstances? For a Zion to be found, a people must arise who will surrender themselves and who are willing to pursue the course upon which God's help can come. There must be people who are there for God, and wholly for God. Even the Savior could not come without a Zion. A man like Simon had to forsake his former ways and gather others around him. A Zacharias had to be found and an Elizabeth, a Hannah, a Joseph, and finally a Mary. They had to be Zion so that the cornerstone could come in which all justice and truth for the future lay hidden. Jesus was born and is now the stone by which we must let ourselves be founded.

Then again, through the disciples a Zion was formed around Jesus. Afterwards, however, Jesus was no longer seen. He died, and he arose, but he ascended to the right hand of God. So how shall things continue now? Jesus would have accomplished nothing if he had not kept a Zion in which he could live, a people who let themselves be governed by him in the Spirit for the glory of God and allowed themselves to be instructed about the establishment of God's justice and truth on the earth. If his disciples had not been of one mind in resisting the world and regarding as empty and useless everything that did not come from above, the name of Jesus would long ago have been forgotten. Without this Zion all would have been in vain, including the empty tomb. The Savior could have gone in glory to the throne of God, and we would have remained unenlightened. It would have been spoken about for a time. But if we merely talk about something, the history of God finally becomes just a quaint story; it takes its place among the legends. That would have been the end of the real life to which these events are meant to bear witness.

Just how much the Savior expects from a Zion is shown by Jesus' prayer in John 17. This prayer shows that nothing will be fulfilled in the world unless people sacrifice themselves for a unity of heart and soul and free themselves entirely from their former life to have in their hearts what is new and perfect. That was the power of God in the apostles. Jesus' disciples were a Zion, prepared for all that God was doing without any consideration of how this or that was possible, or what was reasonable or unreasonable. They had to ask nothing, but only to surrender themselves. So the apostles stand today as a miracle and a sign in the world. A fire of the almighty God proceeded from them, apostolic, not in words, but in power.

Sadly, to a certain extent, this apostolic time came to a sudden end. The apostles died, and gradually this Zion disappeared. Certainly the foundation stone could never be removed from the world. Christ had plowed a deep furrow. There have been devout people ever since. But on the whole, that which is of God has been overrun by human spirits.

Church history does not make for pleasant reading. Early on people began to think, "Are we ready for this or not? Do we want something more or not? No! What we have is enough; after all, we have our faith in Christ, and through him we have salvation. We have a new religion, which has become powerful, surpassing all the others. That is sufficient. We don't need anything more." Through the years the Zion of the apostles has disintegrated into human ideals, and real progress towards the wiping out of the curse of sin and death among the peoples has been frustrated. Christianity has become one more religion. And in this religion people are at a standstill; it is the same old misery of sin and death. Hardly a trace of resurrection and true life reaches into people's lives, makes itself felt physically, or takes form in the here and now. Human cleverness springs up like mushrooms. Human doctrines have become mixed with the truth of Christian faith. Right from the beginning the church fathers had to appear in order to restrain the grossest offenders who called themselves Christian. And as to prophets, there is not a word so much as mentioned anymore.

Without God's Zion all is in vain, including the empty tomb.

Yes, we have "church fathers," but where is the Zion of God? Again and again we have set up human opinions and personal conditions. It is quite striking how these run throughout history right down to the present time. Everyone sets the conditions under which he or she will participate. And Christianity just drifts along quite nicely. But where is the Lion of Judah? Where is the fear of the God who seeks men and women ready to surrender to him without conditions? Once more it is we who rule. In the end weapons have to decide the issues. War and the shedding of blood pave the way for

Christianity, because we humans prevail with our self-will, not the Lion of Judah. He has no Zion.

In the Reformation time a cry for this Zion arose in Luther's soul. He sought a people freely surrendered to God's grace, without self-righteous works, and in this he was right. But what must we say? The clerical element still muddied up the stream of the Reformation. Too many human beings wanted to rule. But Zion is not like this. God's Zion is the fellowship where Christ rules, where we humans do not emerge as a ruling power. If we are to be a Zion, then it is Jesus alone who must rule.

If we expect something new, we must get ready for a Zion. We must prepare our hearts to serve God alone, without regard to any position we may have as members of one or the other denomination. In this way we shall be agents in the forward movement of God. We shall be truly biblical again. For to be biblical is to be free. If we understand this, we will take up a practical attitude. We will not be downhearted and sad when what we have established totters. Instead, we will gladly renounce what we have been doing so far and begin to build a new foundation. Jesus wants to reveal himself by his sovereignty. For this to happen we must accept that our rule must end, wherever and however it exists. We have to surrender ourselves for a new Zion – unconditionally.

If anyone is ready to commit himself, let him lay aside any and every condition. For example, you may say, "Good, I will seek this Zion, but please do not come near me with miracles and signs of God; they are out of place in our time." Yes, dear friend, but if God wants to reveal himself anew, you must be able to surrender yourself for it, no matter how it looks. Others might say, "All knowledge of God is found *only* in the Bible." But with this you strike God directly in the face. Who is Lord? – the Bible, or God? Still others might exclaim, "Yes, I am ready to experience grace, but not God's judgment." But if it is pleasing to God to exercise judgment and to reveal his justice, while you are only ready for some kind of one-sided love, you are setting up a condition. God's Zion smashes to pieces our conditions. This is perhaps the great mistake through which our theologians come to grief, for they record down to the smallest detail what God may or may not legitimately do with us.

Again you make a condition if you say, "I will hold onto this Zion, but can't I also enjoy some peace and quiet?" The time has come when God says, "No! Today you must serve me in trouble! You cannot sit down comfortably in peace when everything is wrong." We cannot sit down peacefully and happily while God's cause is suffering affliction. After all, we are not like the world with its religions. Or are we? We must not settle down in our Christianity, but allow ourselves to be made uneasy so that there may be a true advancement again for God. If God wants to speak to us, do we want to shrink back and say, "No. I don't want that!" Yet that is exactly how we speak. And the Zion of God finds few people.

A new time can be ours if we prepare ourselves in quiet and have hearts that long for a Zion to come into being again. Without Zion there is no clarity. Whoever understands this will surrender himself, not caring for himself but caring for God. He will think: now my whole heart shall be aflame for this, that I become a person with whom God can do what he wants, a person who no longer considers himself at all but considers only the Lord Jesus. Nothing else is of consequence to me if only I may surrender myself to the rule of God. It does not matter if I shall be judged, or if I am already fit to receive God's benefits. One thing only lives in my heart: to give up everything, if it serves him.

There should be an eagerness among us, so much so that each should want to be the first, for on this basis we are "on the racetrack." Everyone runs, one gains the crown. But it does not matter if one is first or last, if only one comes with enthusiasm for God, offering up house and home, wife and child, and everything else in single-hearted fervor that only Jesus may live and rule in all things (1 Cor. 9:24–27). This has to happen. One day all the world will experience the cornerstone. It will happen all the sooner if, whatever their denomination, those who believe in Jesus Christ are on fire for the Zion of God.

We lay foundations that
will need further development. **Oscar Romero**
We provide yeast that produces
effects far beyond our capabilities.

When Jesus saw the young man's mother,
his heart went out to her, and he said,
"Don't cry." Then he went up and touched
the coffin, and those carrying it stood still.
He said, "Young man, I say to you, get up!"
The dead man sat up and began to talk,
and Jesus gave him to his mother.

Luke 7:11–15

11

Not Words, but Deeds

What can we do with a story like this one, where Jesus brings a dead man back to life? What do we do with this when we hear that ten thousand cholera victims are buried in a common grave? And how much more of the miseries of death do we now experience? Where has a dead person ever been raised? So what are we to make of this story? And who among those who believe in Jesus can really find the courage to take an event such as is described here so seriously that

127

he thinks this should also be possible today? For with great sorrow we can ask, where is Jesus, the risen one? Where *is* Jesus in a human race scarred and seared by want and despair?

Is he perhaps hidden in our hearts? Who can say? There must be something of him in the air, so to speak, otherwise we would not hear his name spoken by so many thousands. Nor would we experience the countless number of people who have, in some degree, a longing for Jesus. But if we consider the powers of this Man, we must sorrowfully hang our heads, for we scarcely see any traces of these anymore. The powers of which our Christianity boasts are essentially no different from the powers that are quite customary in the world. We no longer see anything of the Jesus who is Lord over death. This is again and again the cause of all our misery!

We could almost lose heart. If Jesus Christ cannot manifest himself among us as resurrection and life, then we are no different from anyone else. We have no right to look down with disdain on others just because we feel that our beliefs about Jesus are superior to theirs. I say we should instead sink down to the ground in repentance. We should be ashamed that we are not yet people who can experience things such as we read of here in Luke. After all, if there is a God who sent Jesus into the flesh in order that he be proclaimed as the one who rose again from the dead, then it is simply not understandable that this God would want the resurrection and the life-giving deeds of Jesus Christ to be left standing as a mere curiosity in the world – a curiosity that we pass over reverently, but still without being struck by it and without experiencing that Jesus is the resurrection and the life (John 11:25).

Have I a right to preach Jesus, the risen one, when so little changes?

Most Christians comfort themselves with thoughts of "the Last Day." But I say that this looking towards the final resurrection has almost become a slacker's cushion. We Christians are always pushing things off until the second coming of Jesus Christ, until the end of the world. It is almost as if we say to ourselves, "It makes no difference how we die. Everything can remain as it is. We have only to believe and wait until a new world comes." But in this fashion, dear friends, we become people who experience nothing. Then it is no mystery why the Savior, the seed of life, the living seed of resurrection, cannot take root in us and bring forth lasting fruit.

Death, which we often encounter in this or that epidemic, is actually everywhere. However, the germs of disease only become dangerous when they find the right soil to grow in. Then suddenly there are millions upon millions of them, the whole body of a person is infected and within a few hours he lies lifeless, a prey to death.

It is the same in life. Through Jesus we receive stimulation for living. Certainly this can be experienced without having any effect. Just as we often feel a touch of sickness without there being any grounds for death, so we also can feel life-giving impulses without real life gripping us and drawing us into its realm. Thus, especially in our day, we hear of many movements of life springing up in the name of Jesus, but they are short-lived. We actually see nothing of an incisive breakthrough that would make people become alive and bring something new into life. We find very little of this no matter where we look. And for this reason I sometimes have to ask myself if I am even entitled to speak a word about Jesus. This is often the greatest temptation for me. I often think, how can I even read this story? Have I a right to preach Jesus, the risen one, when so little changes? For where can I see or experience anything of this? Even if many stirrings of life are to be felt, there is nothing which one could call "rising from the dead." There are not even isolated instances of which one could say, "See, that is Jesus, the risen one."

In light of this, our views and opinions are completely unimportant. They are ridiculous in comparison to what actually happens. Compared to what happens, our beliefs and views have been blown up to monstrous proportions. Some embrace a "Blumhardt view" of Jesus the victor, who performs miracles and raises up the dead, while others hold that Blumhardt is a fool. Still others maintain that what the Bible describes is all nonsense, all in the past. In short, different Christian viewpoints dominate, and what actually takes place is left completely behind, so much so that the most significant things are argued away into oblivion.

The mania for opinions, for different interpretations, is so great among us that we very easily dismiss even the most powerful occurrences. On innumerable occasions it has happened to me that when I try to impart what I have seen of the resurrection, I am told: "Oh, that can be explained differently. That also happens in the hospitals; everyone experiences that." Such a barrier has been erected in people's minds, even among Christians, that whether or not it is expressed or admitted, we live as if such things can never happen. If this is the case, then one can well ask, "Have we a right to preach Jesus?" Do you think it is a pleasure to give to people some little treasure-trove from the Bible, a nice little explanation of a text, for example? If only God would grant that I had nothing more to say, that I had no understanding of the Bible and interested nobody with my ideas about it. If only God would grant that I knew nothing of theology, but simply had demonstrations and proofs of true life (1 Thess. 1:5). Jesus would be revealed more clearly to the simple, to those who hunger and thirst! Jesus does not want to renew the world through ideas but through deeds.

People think that Death is something dead. No! Death is something "alive."

Oh, how I would be satisfied if you could only grasp this one point. Jesus has become the subject of so many interpretations, and it is these that have caused the terrible need we are in. Therefore I long so much that you could count everything as loss in order to gain the living Christ, including all you have learned, all that you feel, and all the ideas and notions that concern and stir you (Phil. 3:7–11). I dare to contend, and I will contend with the last drop of my blood, that Jesus is completely different from what everyone holds him to be today. What people think of him is sheer loss, and what they do with him can lead to the greatest ruin. They push people into theories about Jesus, and in the process his living reality is lost. Jesus is put to death even by the devout, who, mind you, especially do not want to hear me say this. But I maintain, and will continue to maintain in the face of every opposition, that Jesus is completely different from what is proclaimed to us today! He is a man of deeds, of God's deeds, not the topic of discussions. There are miracles today just as in that time, for Jesus is the risen one today just as he was then (John 14:12). Whoever truly believes in him will see this to be true – something to be experienced. And if a person does not believe this, then despite the most believing opinion of Jesus, such a person does not yet grasp the 'A' of the alphabet of who Jesus is. He kills Jesus along with all the others who kill him with their unbelief.

But what do we do now, dear friends? People will say to me, "You can talk as much as you like, but tomorrow you will be dead, and you will also be forgotten!" Therefore I will not stop with this. The story we have heard is not simply something to be marveled at. It is not about beautiful ideas of rising from the dead, but about something practical. It must make an impact on us here and now, or we are lost!

In this connection, let us recall the gospel story about the young man from the town of Nain. This account speaks of the terrible oppression by the scribes and Pharisees, and of how they wanted to silence the message of Jesus. Yet in spite of this, Jesus' influence, his breath of life, penetrated into the house of a certain widow. She was timid and surrounded her son with motherly care, but her son burned more and more to meet Jesus. With the genuine, intense enthusiasm that young people often have, he thought, I want to meet this Jesus! What a man he must be! How much we hear about him. He could not sleep without dreaming of his desire to come near to this man. This was wildly alive in him and almost consumed him, for he did not know how to bring this about.

Then the young man died. And when they carried out his body and encountered Jesus, his famished spirit was appeased and he simply had to live again. He was, so to speak, infected by Jesus. Now as Jesus approached him, the whole life of Jesus the Son of God took hold of the young man. The soil had been prepared, and whether science can account for it or not, he sat up.

If we want to experience the risen one, if we are eagerly waiting for the coming one, then we must also do our part. There must be something in us that can rise to meet this Jesus when he comes. And then, whether we are physically dead or alive, we shall arise. Whether we are in the body or outside the body, we shall live. But there must be a seed, however tiny, which is fully prepared to rise up and meet Jesus when he approaches us.

I do not mean to say that we should pray for lots of miracles to happen. No, such things do not happen to dead people, not to really dead people in whom nothing at all lives. No, what is most important is that there is something alive, something genuine and whole on this earth. We must allow ourselves to be infected by the living presence of Christ now, or else God's deeds will never come. For this Savior of ours really wants to be among us in resurrection and life – in actual fact and not just in our heads. Then perhaps, just as with the young man, this will so fill our hearts that it will overflow in longing for that which God's honor seeks.

If you grasp what I am saying, then you must and will get completely away from yourselves. For this is not to be mixed up with our own personal desires and longings. Our longings in regard to miracles are completely secondary. The only valid desire is to see Jesus the Christ, to meet him, because he has come from the Father and is coming again. Only one desire is important: that the power and nature of Jesus may again take shape upon earth and be seen once more, whether in me or in a Chinese person, or in whomever. It does not matter at all. The main thing is that Jesus is again understood for what he is. This desire, this fervency of heart, must live in us (Heb. 12:1–3). Without this, we remain dead. In this fervency we must forget ourselves and desire only God's deeds, only Jesus' rulership, only the spirit of life, in sickness, temptation, and tribulations of all kinds. This is the practical reality of resurrection I am getting at: sigh and long for this Jesus!

It is not a matter of nursing "dead" people, but a matter of us all becoming new people.

People think that Death is something dead. No! Death is a bacteria; it is alive and finds soil everywhere in which to propagate itself. It kills not only the body but often, long before this, spirit and soul. Death is something "alive," and this life of death is something you need to recognize more and more. I will not say too much about it. Perhaps some of you have felt something of this for a long time already. It is something each one must feel and come to know for himself. I can only hint at how much is alive that comes from death.

When we feel this, however, we will indeed know that it is Jesus we need, for no dogma, no system, no ideology can kill this bacteria of Death. No matter what we are taught religiously in school or at home, even if we learn to repeat word for word different verses from the Bible, the forces of death are not, as a result, destroyed. We must be filled with a much more glowing heat, hotter than all the heat with which we are able to kill the bacilli of sickness. And we can obtain this heat, this ardor, when we distinguish between the things of heaven and the things of this world, between the life of death and the life of God. Truly, the person who perceives this distinction can, with all the ardor of his heart, long that Jesus, the only possibility of salvation from this life of death, may appear once more. I can't understand why people do not give up everything else! I cannot understand why people do not have a glowing, burning desire for this Jesus to appear. Only by the boiling heat of longing for God's deeds, only in fervent expectation, can the life of death be killed.

May the Lord give us strength that we do not become weary, and may Jesus himself purify us (1 John 3:3). But a fight lies before us and I must say this, even if I am the only one to express it like this: the very life of Jesus is the main issue in the world. There is nothing else that matters. We must persevere in the battle for the living Christ and become ever more ardent in our desire to gain only this Christ, and nothing else. For Christ is completely different from the Jesus of our churches and of our opinions. If we can persevere in this glowing heat of longing we can then experience a little of the death of Death. We shall also experience that the streams of God's future, the life to come, will flow through to all the peoples of the world. Oh, how small and trivial will our present condition appear to be then! It is not a matter of improvement; it is a matter of renewal. Not a matter of nursing "dead" people, but a matter of us all becoming new people. May God grant that we experience this!

We cannot do everything, and there is a sense of liberation in realizing that.

Oscar Romero

I want to know Christ
and the power of his resurrection
and the fellowship of his sufferings,
becoming like him in his death,
and so, somehow, to attain to the
resurrection from the dead.

Philippians 3:10–11

Christ Is Rising

Only when we have personally encountered Christ have we entered into a new world. We must actually come to Christ, and not just through the motions of coming to him, reading about him in the Bible and saying, "He is a fine teacher, and he says such good and beautiful things; I am going to try hard to do them, and I'm going to stick with him. He's a good man, or even God's Son." We can do all that and this might well make us a certain kind of good Christian. But more than that has to happen. Our hearts and minds have to be lifted to another sphere altogether (Col. 3:1–4), where we can live and arrange life on an entirely different basis.

It is easy to wonder how people will ever become different. Everything humanly possible seems so miserably inadequate. Anything we do to change the values or morals of some group of people or other does not seem in the least to have any effect. We live before a great black background out of which horrible forces keep rising and making human beings so inhuman that they sink below the level of beasts. Even with all our civilization, all our technological know-how – and I do not want to belittle the advantages of these – human nature on the whole is wrapped in great darkness.

But, dear friends, our hope never has been built on human ideas. Every time that has been tried, it has failed. Our hope rests on the fact that there is one who rose from the dead, that he is sitting at the right hand of God and lives now in the power of God (Heb. 10:12). In this power he rules and will judge. He is victor. True, all that is earthly is still engulfed in weakness. Jesus too had to suffer all the limitations of human life. However, he is risen. He is no longer buried in these human things. He rises up healthy and whole out of all the darkness and appears to us as the shining, glorious Lord, full of power and life, the power to give life to others, no matter how thick the darkness that surrounds him.

This is the form the resurrection takes, the resurrection we want to know by the power of God. The resurrection does not consist solely of what happened in the past, nor does it consist of what we happen to believe dogmatically about it – those are not the essential things. We do not gain much by just accepting that Christ died and rose again. Many people believe this, but nevertheless they go to hell. This belief is of no help unless you and I experience Jesus as Lord. It is not the worst if some people are unable to believe that Christ rose from the dead – at least they still regard it as something tremendous, too tremendous to glibly confess. The sad thing is that so many people today claim to believe it, and yet it means so little to them. It has no effect in their lives. But there is resurrection today just as much as there was back then, after Christ's death. There is resurrection – for with a certain part of our inner being we can be in a completely different place, where most people don't dare to go. Our renewal is real to the extent that we find ourselves in an entirely different order.

It is not enough to accept that Christ died and rose again. Many people go to hell believing this.

A person who is with Christ will not push the world away. Neither will he let himself be embittered by the way people are, no matter what they are like (1 Cor. 5:9–10). He isn't offended by the horrors of sin. Instead, he is like a child who feels that he can already rejoice that there are divine powers, divine thoughts, and a divine spirit, all different from the influences that we happen to meet here on earth. The one who is in Christ experiences the tremendous abundance and variety of these divine powers, and is so filled with the sense of them that it is natural to live by them. Indeed these powers of life can come to us, powers that other people would never think possible. That is what it means to be risen with Christ. That is what we should be, not for our own good but for the world's good, for the good of other people, for those we live with and even suffer from. Therefore, we do not push away the world. We assert our place in the midst of it, and we hold our place right among the sons of men – the poorest and lowest of all – trusting that everything can still be different because of the work of the divine powers that we experience.

And so our task is to know the power of the resurrection, that power that alone is in Christ. You can look to many human powers. Here and there you can find something of beauty and something relatively good, but all of it is maimed, and it is powerless to overcome the evils in this world. We must look to a higher life, to a mightier power that cannot be found among people at this time, power that is not at all of this world. This extraordinary strength, this amazing vitality that appears only in the God who is revealed in Christ, is the power that must be pulled out of the invisible regions into visibility. This power is not so very far away because in Christ, God has become flesh. Again and again Christ arises anew. In what we know of the risen Christ, God wants to renew all things. His will is for the earth as much as it is for the heavens. Otherwise we would never know his reality. We could never conceive of anything becoming different. We would think that his resurrected life was some spiritual thing that we human beings could not understand. That's not what it is. No. The power of his resurrection is something that is within our reach.

We do not push away the world. We assert our place in it.

New possibilities can dawn on us, and the more we sense these new possibilities, either in our bodies or in our souls, the more we can ask for, the more we can look for higher and greater things here on earth. Actually, there are no limits. And for this reason we can bring hope into everything, into our daily life, into everything at which we work and into anything that we touch. The power that comes from God is ready to be brought into our human situation, and in such a way as to transform it.

Therefore, we must not turn our attention to the darkness, the evils, and the imperfections of the earth, nor are we to try to figure out how this or that matter is going to turn out. All that has nothing to do with us. We are simply to ask Jesus to give us more and more of his resurrection, until it runs over, until the extraordinary powers from on high that are within our reach can get down to work on all that we do.

We can spoil the deeds of God if we think they rely on us.

If we pursue the higher goals among humanity by the usual methods or even with extraordinary works of love, we have no hope of accomplishing anything. In every case where we want to help someone along, strength has to come from Christ. Yes, this places us in a sort of concealment. God cannot appear openly in the world, at least not as it is today. Things will not become that obvious. There are those who are in contact with Christ, who are in some way acquainted with higher powers, but these powers remain concealed within them, as they did in Christ incarnate. Only the eyes of faith are able to recognize the power of God at work.

Those who think everything has to be done by ways and means, who think that we have to call on human understanding to determine what to do against all the darkness of the world, are wrong (Eph. 6:10–18). If that is the way we are supposed to approach things, we are beaten. We will never make the world Christian by what we have done or with what we may yet accomplish. We can spoil the deeds that come from the strength of God if we think they depend on the strength that comes from us. For our part, the word for us is, "Seek! Strive for the things above!" This is made hard because we must do so in quiet. But it is the strongest power we have if we would but stand before God and say, "Dear

Father in heaven, reveal your strength. Give us your strength for every day, for every year, for all times. I shall live for you alone. Let us keep experiencing the powers from above, the new life, the power that enables you to bring everything under your control (Phil. 3:21). Let the resurrection of Christ's life in us go on becoming stronger and mightier until the moment when his glory is revealed."

That is our work. We need do nothing but go on living in gladness, confident that there are new powers available for those who believe. Then power from God will be drawn into life through us and through all who have experienced the resurrection. Therefore we who have experienced something of these higher powers of God, whether in health or behavior, should be loyal and not give up hope at any point. We need no longer look at the black side of things, but instead can look to the resurrection and allow it to be the most important reality in our life. We should keep striving for nothing else. Then we are able to help bring on the time when Christ will be revealed in his glory.

This enables us
to do something and
to do it very well.

**Oscar
Romero**

I will bless the Lord at all times,
his praise will always be on my lips.
My soul will boast in the Lord;
let the afflicted hear and rejoice.
Glorify the Lord with me;
let us exalt his name together.

Psalm 34:1–3

13

What Do You Stand For?

I will bless the Lord at all times," exclaims the psalmist. These words from scripture are not just pleasant, pious words to be recited in ease and comfort. For Israel, this verse was a battle cry born out of need and temptation: "The angel of the Lord encamps around those who fear him, and he delivers them…The lions may grow weak and hungry, but those who seek the Lord lack no good thing" (Ps. 34:7–9).

Israel had experienced the Lord as a mighty God of justice. He had used his power, for example, to lead his people to justice and truth, vanquishing Egypt. With great mercy, compassion, and kindness he had delivered his people from Pharaoh's clutches in order to establish them as a blessing for the nations. Like a mother with her children, he had settled them to rest and fed them, and under his leadership they were led into the desert.

Naturally they could not go on forever being waited on hand and foot. Israel was to be judged and had to take much upon itself. Israel had to suffer privations – go to school, as it were – and outgrow its faults (Gal. 4:1–7). The God of justice and truth does not adapt himself to the conventional life patterns of nations and societies. He does not want his people to live as other nations (Deut. 10:12–22) nor to copy the manners and customs of others and gradually sink into all the foolish nonsense of mankind, as if that is happiness. His people are to be an emphatically different people.

This, of course, is uncomfortable, and as a result grumblers and rebels were always to be found among the people of Israel (Exod. 16). At times these became so numerous that it no longer seemed wrong to erect temples of foreign nations, even in Israel, and to express piety in a heathen way. Was that not religion too? And wasn't any religion better than none at all? But for the God of justice no "religion" was acceptable, let alone such a wicked one. This did not suit the people. It seemed terrible that what all the other people considered good, all that made them strong and through which they had achieved great civilizations, was to be called wrong. So they grumbled and complained and finally lost their peace with God. Yet there were also people who said, "I will praise the Lord. I will strive to put into practice what we have experienced as justice and truth. Even if everyone else should grumble and rebel I say, 'I will bless the Lord at all times. His praise shall continually be on my lips.'"

In Israel there were such fighters, and such fighters we also have to be. For it also happens today that everything that God demands of us is uncomfortable, and what we have made for ourselves and become accustomed to must be overthrown. Among us, too, God finds plenty of grumbling and defiance.

Today a judgment is being passed upon our age. A finger of truth points to this or that lie or error in traditions and religions. A finger of justice demands that we follow the voice of conscience and consider what must be changed. When human generations live on for decades without being shaken and stirred up by the powerful flood of events in history, then their customs and traditions can become too cozy and too comfortable. In the end these very human constructions take the place

God's finger of justice demands that we follow the voice of conscience.

of God. Then it happens that we are only concerned about defending our human institutions. It seems as if everything will collapse if the institutions that have grown up over the years are overturned. Consequently, we are often too cowardly to stand up for God's justice. We ignore the deficiencies and wrong things and become used to them so that just about anything is tolerated. We keep allowing things to go on as usual. It does not matter how much wrong there is or how many groan under it. When a voice of godly justice arises to call for what is true and right, it is reviled and repudiated and the foolishness defended.

But we have to keep in mind that our God, as revealed in Jesus Christ, is a God of justice and a God of truth – not a God of politics, society, tradition, church, school, or denomination. These may have value. But we have proof enough that they can and do go wrong. Even long-standing institutions, which may have been relatively good at first but which have gradually failed to fulfill their purpose, will have to be opposed. This also applies to the religious life. God himself brings about changes. These changes frequently cause great discomfort (Matt. 10:34). Nevertheless, if we want to serve God we will have to acknowledge what is true and just.

In our restless age in which society, as well as customs and traditions, is changing, we must keep only one thing in mind: the God of justice. We have to be a free people. We have to become so free that we can believe that everything might change radically. For the God of justice is here. The God of truth is victorious over all that is dead and decaying. Those who worship him will do so in spirit and in truth (John 4:23–24).

If we become such a people, then no swirling current of the future will sweep us away. In deep quiet we will reach the eternal rock. And on this rock Christ will prove his unconquerable cause. All our denominations and divisions dishonor God. The time must come when we will no longer seek to stand before God, the king, with any piety other than truthfulness and justice in our heart. Jesus, the Lord of truth, will sweep away everything human from this earth, no matter how good it may seem to us. Because, in the end, the kingdom of God does not separate us into various groups as we have had them up to now. It will come in a form where the only questions are: What are you fighting for? Will you make a stand for what is right – not for your party or for your church, but for the truth that will make our life different than before?

This has great significance in the vicissitudes of life to which we are exposed. Here too we find many who grumble and are defiant. If things do not go well with them, then God and the world are at fault. The world has to carry the blame when they run into trouble. But

it is just here that a real fighter will prove himself.
Whoever blames God or the world when he or she is in
trouble, does not say, "I will bless the Lord at all times.
His praise shall continually be in my mouth." But if
someone takes the guilt upon himself and remembers
that we mortals are not yet standing on the ground of
righteousness and truth and that is why we have to suffer, such a person will become strong-hearted and will
be able to say, "We want to bring about the justice of
our God. This is what we want to stand for, also spe-
cifically, in all that befalls humankind." If we would
cease to pity, defend, and excuse ourselves, but rather
consider where we have failed when we find ourselves
in entangled situations, if we would keep the certainty
in our hearts that God and the world are not to blame
but that the fault lies with us, then we will be a people
ready for the kingdom of God, clearing the way for the
coming of God's justice and truth.

Let us never forget that an enormously large part of
the world is just a human fabrication. We are capable
of creating for ourselves all kinds of worlds. We can
make ourselves a philosophical world, or a social world,
or a national world. We can also create a pious world
for ourselves, and a Christian world. This world of our
own creation is certainly not God's world. If we look at
it squarely, we will see that the guilt is our own, even
when exceptional influences of evil bring us into need

and misery. A world of sin has grown up alongside the world of God. This world exists and is ruled by our human spirit. In so far as we love this world of our own creation, this world of people and nations and their history and tradition, we cannot see God's world. To the extent that we want to hold on to our own world and put our own ideas and wishes at the center, we will not see what is of God nor find the real foundation of his justice.

God is a God of justice and truth – not a God of politics or church.

It is this tragic self-righteousness, this living without true fear of God, that finally leads to our not being able to see God's rulership. It is all because of the worlds we have created. And the ramifications of this are to be seen in all areas of life. There are all sorts of little worlds in which people become stuck without having considered whether such a world comes from God. Their whole being is so wrapped up in their own world that they can only see God through a mist of their own creation. This is how it comes about that today certain people, even preeminently religious people, live in their own world and despise the essence of God. And it can happen that because we can no longer see what is true – because of the world we ourselves have created – we drive out what is right. Do you think God exists solely for the sake of upholding our world? Far from it! He wants none of our deceitfulness. And then people make a big to-do about God being love, just as if this dear

God were obliged to support our human foolishness out of love in order to keep his dear children from having to suffer. Such people completely forget that God's love is the love of justice, a love of truth and not a love of deceptions!

Therefore let us pull ourselves together without complaining and without obstinacy. Our own worlds will collapse. They will not last. But, praise God, we can rejoice when these fleshly human worlds fall, as long as we hold on firmly to the God of justice even as they collapse and do not allow ourselves to be in the least bit turned aside from striving for the world of God. Such an attitude of heart and such a striving of our spirit will lead us to experience the forward movement of the kingdom of God.

A short time ago I met someone and, during the course of our conversation, we touched briefly upon the subject of religion. He immediately came out with, "There is no progress in religion. That is our experience. It is always the same. Religion stands still." I was shocked, but I had to say, "Yes, you are right!" But there is progress in the truth and truth is concerned with life and justice. No technical advances can bring about progress in life, nor will they make us human beings just and true. But there is progress in the kingdom of God.

So we must not lose heart. Let us bless the Lord at all times. We must expend ourselves on the foundation of the coming kingdom of God, and not cling to this or that petty concern. For in the end all human works will be transfigured by his divine breath, so that if they are good and worthy they may be purified and stand forever. Or, if they are bad, they shall be destroyed without grace or mercy. For all that is unjust will pass away, but what is right and true will endure forever.

It may be incomplete, but it is a beginning, a step along the way, an opportunity for God's grace to enter and do the rest.

Oscar Romero

> Be dressed for action
> and have your lamps lit;
> be like those who are waiting
> for their master to return
> from the wedding banquet,
> so that they may open
> the door for him as soon
> as he comes and knocks.
>
> Luke 12:35–36

14

Get Ready for Action

You must not be surprised if our hearts are not exactly lit in regard to the coming of God. To us it is like a treasure whose value is appreciated by only a few and in which most people take only a passing interest. Of course, there are many today who sigh to heaven, "Savior, come now!" But they are not sighing for the sake of God's kingdom. They cry out like this only when they are in trouble and want God to help them. And

163

they don't know of any help that is more effective than to have a Savior come and put a quick end to their troubles.

This makes it hard for anyone who seeks to be a part of God's plan and who wants to work for it. When it comes to the things of God we are not to be concerned for what is ours, but only to be concerned for what belongs to Jesus Christ. We should do this not merely for our own edification; we must become workers for God. This leads us to God's vineyard, a place where there is not a great deal of talk, but where everyone is intent on deeds.

Let us concentrate then on the experience that equips us to act, not according to our human plans, but according to God's plan:

> Be ready for action, and have your lamps lit; be like those who are waiting for their master to return from the wedding banquet, so that they may open the door for him as soon as he comes and knocks. Blessed are those slaves whom the master finds alert when he comes; truly I tell you, he will fasten his belt and have them sit down to eat, and he will come and serve them. If he comes during the middle of the night or near dawn and finds them ready, blessed are those slaves.
>
> But know this: if the owner of the house had known at what hour the thief was coming, he would

not have let his house be broken into. You also must be ready, for the Son of Man is coming at an unexpected hour.

Peter said, "Lord, are you telling this parable for us or for everyone?" and the Lord said, "Who then is the faithful and prudent manager whom his master will put in charge of his slaves, to give them their allowance of food at the proper time? Blessed is the slave whom his master will find at work when he arrives. Truly I tell you, he will put that one in charge of all his possessions. But if that slave says to himself, 'My master is delayed in coming,' and if he begins to beat the other slaves, men and women, and to eat and drink and get drunk, the master of that slave will come on a day when he does not expect him and at an hour that he does not know, and will tear him to pieces and put him with the unfaithful. That slave who knew what his master wanted but did not prepare himself or do what was wanted, will receive a severe beating. But the one who did not know and did what deserved a beating will receive a lesser beating. From everyone to whom much has been given, much will be required; and from the one to whom much has been entrusted, even more will be demanded" (Luke 12:35–48).

In God's vineyard there is not a great deal of talk; everyone is intent on deeds.

Here Jesus is speaking of his disciples and their preparation for his coming. Take note that God's kingdom is not formed by any human discovery or intention, however daring and noble, nor by anything other than the coming of Christ. Our faith, our ardor, must be for this coming. Otherwise it would be better to put aside our meditations on the kingdom of God. The reign of God is a marvelous thing. To worldly wisdom God's kingdom seems like foolishness, and yet it gives shape to the whole world, the whole creation, making it God's eternal creation.

It is remarkable that not only God, creator of heaven and earth, but also God's people must be a part of this plan. There need to be men and women who give themselves up for God's kingdom and its justice and truth as it is to be on earth. Otherwise Jesus would not have said, "Blessed are those servants whom the master finds awake when he comes." And he certainly would not have said that he will serve such people. It is obvious that much depends on their activity. We can even read between the lines that if no people are there to watch out, God's coming will be delayed. Speaking in terms of the parable, if the doorkeeper does not open the door, it is possible that even the master himself, who has given him the key, cannot get in unless he forces his way.

There have to be people who, first of all, have dressed themselves for action and have lit their lamps. In other words, while their master is absent they are busy preparing everything in the house for his arrival and keeping everyone in the house aware that the state they are living in is only temporary.

Secondly, there must be people who stand by the door and listen for him and who open it quickly when he knocks. Workers, not slackers, are dressed for service. Slackers wear their Sunday best. A person who is getting ready to work with his hands takes his coat off and rolls up his sleeves so that he can get at the matter without further ado. God has work that has to be done in work clothes, not in one's Sunday best. In fact, we must never think of Sunday clothes as normal. Such a notion makes one's personal piety and devotion for the satisfaction of one's own needs the only important thing. As long as God's kingdom has to be fought for, it is more important to be dressed for work – ready for action – to make an effort to do something in keeping with God's plan, often against the whole weight of the world. A practical way exists that supports the truth and justice of God's kingdom, and we must be ready for this with our whole being.

But, someone may ask, "What sort of thing, exactly, are we to do? What will truly serve God and his kingdom?" That is a serious question; no human being can answer it. We have to learn to live in what is coming from God every day and to carry a light from this awareness into the darkness. For the essence of God's

God's work is to be done in work clothes, not in Sunday best.

**Let your-
self be led
to places
where you
would never
go of your
own accord.**

everlasting order has been darkened by the principali-
ties and powers of this world. Throughout practically
every realm of life there is an enslaving force. It is characteristic of everything, even the highest human un-
dertakings of nations or of individuals; it is egoism.
What will we get out of a thing for our own momen-
tary interest? Anything that is in our own immediate
interest, this we call good and true. In this way the darkness comes, a darkness in which no one can do anything unless he carries a light illuminated by God.

Basically, as soon as it is a matter of putting God's
service into our daily life, we weak human beings don't
really know, or want to know, what is true. We live in a
mass of wrongs and untruths, and they surround us as
a dark, dark night. Not even in the most flagrant things
do we manage to break through. We are hardly repelled
anymore by murder, adultery, or theft. We now have
customs and laws under whose protection one person
can kill another. We have lifestyles of pleasure that poi-
son everything way beyond human help. We have customs of acquisitiveness by which some people live at
the expense of others. What can be done to help?

So many, many people do all sorts of things that are
wrong without having the remotest idea that they are
doing so. Good people, many of them highly esteemed,
people with good hearts, try to do good and yet they

fail to put a stop to the wrongs that confront them, whether in their own lives or in the lives of others.

Anyone whose attention is fixed on the coming reign of God and who wants to see a change brought about in God's house will become more and more aware that a universal wrongness of things is pulled over us like a choking, suffocating blanket. He will know that the thing to do is to take hold of God's hand so that there is some effect on this night, so that at least a few areas are made receptive to God's truth and justice and are made ready to receive God himself. But to do this work we have to have a light. With this light we can then illuminate every corner where we have some work to do. Then we will see where the garbage is, where there is work to be done.

This is really very hard work. For when someone holds a light in his hand and shines it here and there, he is immediately asked, "What business have you here?" So gradually many people let their light go out again. It is too awkward, too inconvenient to keep holding up a light and showing people the dirt and saying, "There, clean that up; the way you are doing things now isn't right in God's eyes. Cut off your hand! Tear out your eye! Cut off your foot!" – as Jesus says, figuratively, when there is something about the hand or eye or foot that stands in God's way.

That is what is meant by letting your light shine. A light has a purpose; a light ought to shine into our conditions so that we can see what needs to be done and set our hand to it and clean it up. Jesus, with this light, was not well received, and neither were his apostles. "If only that light weren't there," people said. In the times of the early church, the Christians were accused of causing confusion in the world, of undermining law and religion, and they were bitterly persecuted for this. The truth – the fact that people's lives are not right – is too much for most people to grasp. It seems like a crime to them to think that things they consider quite all right ought to be changed. The sacrifice of Christ, which makes it possible for a new humanity to arise in the resurrection – this sacrifice appears as foolishness.

So people turn finally to this Sunday religion. Going to worship is supposed to be enough. God is supposed to be satisfied with it and do without the weekday work. But let us not give the name of worship, or service to God, only to things that benefit us, only to things that soothe our own souls. You are allowed to have much; God is kind. He lets you make many demands on him for your salvation. But then it should also occur to you to let God make demands on you, to let yourself be bound and led to places where you would never go of your own accord. Yes, I will let the light shine for me, but I will do so only to show where there is work to be done for God, where my own happiness does not come into the picture.

Many will answer to this, "Just look at him! Now we're supposed to do good works frantically again. Where does faith come in? He talks like a Catholic." And they say other things as people do who always want to be wearing their Sunday clothes. But no matter how people talk, work clothes must come back.

Fortunately, many people no longer feel that Sunday religion is enough. A new spirit is awakening, and there are many who seek for God's advantage, even though they may not know how to go about it. Others may polish themselves up spiritually to get their little souls in order for God. They can do this, but it is not enough. Anyone who has eyes will see this and consider how he can forget himself in devotion to God's kingdom and become ardent for the kingdom to come – to this he is called.

Closely connected with this first work is that of standing at the door and opening it. In regard to this work one often speaks of the first, second, or third watch; and, I would like to add, the fourth, the fifth, and the sixth. We must stand by constantly, even though there may be no knock for a long time. Jesus' resurrection means that everything in God's kingdom is alive; in every moment there is something happening.

He himself has not yet come, but he may soon send

a messenger to knock. When the door is opened he will say, "Listen, do this and that; tell the people in the house to watch out for this or that." Another time there is another knock, and the door is opened. This time perhaps the word is, "What is the foolishness you're doing in this house? You act as if things were going to always stay the same. Don't settle down as if you were the masters!" And this goes like the breath of God's wrath through the whole house, by way of the doorkeeper. Another time there is a knock, the doorkeeper opens, and the warning is heard, "Watch out for idolatry! Do you want to serve both God and mammon? Do you want to sit at both God's table and the demons' table? Who is your master? Do you want to work with the methods of this world or by the spirit of God? Truly, my house is not a house of human wisdom, but of God's."

For those who listen for Christ's future, a knock sounds over and over again. The things that come forth are not necessarily highly spiritual. Sometimes they are very simple things. For instance, we may be told, "Don't neglect your bodies. Don't you know that your body is a temple of the Holy Spirit? (1 Cor. 3:16) Why do you drink so much wine? Why do you eat so much food?" This seems contemptibly small. Doesn't Paul say, "The kingdom of God does not consist in eating and drinking?" That is true. Yet for those who want to hear, there is a knock on the door for the future of Jesus Christ telling us to live for God in everything (1 Cor. 10:31). It is not only your souls that matter, but your bodies too. How can you find truth in your soul if your body lives in falsehood? Whoever is wise will open the door when God's messengers speak about this. Whoever is wise will go at it joyfully and confidently.

We must speak in practical terms. Either Christ's future has meaning for us now, or else it means nothing at all. Sometimes the knock has to do with our life together, or with the arrangements of our life in relationship to the world. For example, on a large estate there are managers, farmers, gardeners, cooks, and so on. The cook has learned cooking, the farmer farming, the gardener gardening, all according to the customary methods. They have learned their trades well and are able to carry them on, even to excel in them. But suppose there is a knock, the door is opened and they are told, "Listen now, don't simply keep house as the world does; stop and think how to do things so as to please me!" Maybe you will answer, "What do you mean? That's the way I learned it and that's how everybody else does it." True, everybody does it that way; but you do not need to. Those intent on Christ's coming have to bring a different way into their situations. Must things al-

If you look for the truth in small matters, you won't go astray in big ones.

ways be done in the style of the world? (2 Cor. 10:3–4)
According to human wisdom? Should the kingdom of
God run according to what most of us are used to?

A person who keeps watch for God will be glad to
hear even about little things like this, even if he is told,
"Do everything differently from the way you have been
doing it till now." When such a person hears the hint
to do it differently, he will stop and listen. He will ask,
"Differently? How shall I do it differently?" First you
will have to become poor and see where you have acted
foolishly, like someone who has no light. Then you must
grieve that you are not any cleverer than anyone else
when it comes to opening the door to the Master.

This is what it means to watch. We have to begin
with what we can see. Then there will come times when
we are allowed to watch in higher things. If you look
for the truth in small matters you will not go astray in
big ones. You will be able to recognize truth there and
carry out the command that comes. Let us keep staunch
in our eagerness to do whatever comes to us of the truth.
Then there will be knocks on our door, over and over,
and God's coming will not be hidden. For devoted hearts
the light will keep dawning from him who is merciful
and compassionate.

But if we go about our work of watching in pride
and groan, "Oh dear, there's that knocking again. We

just had everything so nicely arranged and now it has to be changed again" – then no lasting work will ever be done. No more knocks will come to our doors. We might as well do as we please until the Lord comes. But then we will get quite a shock; it will be like a thief taking everything out of our hands.

The work of the doorkeeper and the watchman goes together with the work of those who are dressed, ready for action. Unless you stand at the door and watch, dressed ready for action, you will fall asleep before you know it. But if you are dressed and ready for service, you will receive a light from God, and with its help you will be able to discern God's will and carry it out. The work for God goes on quite simply in this way; one does not always have to wait for something out of the ordinary. The all-important thing is to keep your eyes on what comes from God and to make way for it to come into being here on the earth. If you always try to be heavenly and spiritually minded, you won't understand the everyday work God has for you to do. But if you embrace what is to come from God, if you live for Christ's coming in practical life, you will learn that divine things can be experienced here and now, things quite different from what our human brains can ever imagine.

We can be heavenly servants even now, through toil and work, through difficulty and need, through

affliction, fear, and pain. All these things must be overcome by watching. Don't let your hope be stolen from
you. In this hope, make yourselves free for God's will
and God's ways on earth.

We may never see the end results, but that is the difference between the master builder and the worker.

Oscar Romero

The Jews gathered around Jesus, saying,
"How long will you keep us in suspense?
If you are the Christ, tell us plainly."
Jesus answered, "I did tell you, but you
do not believe. The miracles I do in
my father's name speak for me, but
you do not believe because you are not
my sheep. My sheep listen to my voice;
I know them, and they follow me."

John 10:22–30

Don't Push – Surrender!

In the kingdom of God impatience can make people blind and lead them tragically astray. All the good things that we strive for and hope for from God can be taken away from us when we give in to this failing and are impatient.

The root of our impatience lies in our compulsion to achieve. Nothing motivates us more than being asked to do something in keeping with our strength, our ability. Just the pledge to do something, to improve a situation, can excite thousands of people. Even sensible people waver and get carried away. They think, yes, we must and we can do something! And when this human element enters many people in the Kingdom begin to act on their own. God is not fast enough for them, and they rush ahead and press forward according to their own understanding. They also want leaders, if they can find such, to whom they can subordinate themselves and whom they can follow with enthusiasm. Then human strength is roused, in spite of all the misery, all the failure, all the sin that we know is there.

The kingdom of God, however, comes in an entirely different way. It makes no call upon human strength or the exertions of the flesh. The kingdom of God makes us quiet – and for us this is the hardest thing. To have to see that we ourselves are powerless when it comes to the most important affairs of our lives and in attaining the highest goals, and that we must drop all our powers, good as well as bad, is the hardest thing for us to do (Jer. 9:23–24). Again and again impatience rears up in our hearts like a dragon. In fact, it is almost a rebellion against the living God because we, in comparison to him, are nothing at all.

Concerning this impatience we can thank a great deal of bad education and a great number of spiritual miscarriages. Let us remember this, dear friends. Let us be aware that we too could easily cry out against God and against Christ, "How long will you hold us back? Let us move ahead!" And silently, secretly, the words ring within our hearts: "We want to be great people! We want to brandish the sword! We want to become men and women of renown! We want a battle cry with which to storm the world – and you hold us back! If you are the Christ, tell us!"

The root of impatience lies in our compulsion to achieve.

Does God hold back souls in the kingdom of God? Yes, yes, always! He holds back those who want to go forward on their own strength and who want to justify their flesh by their own zeal. He holds back those who would like to bring all their old nature with them into the kingdom of God and to be praised because they are the driving force, because they are the people who advance the cause. God holds back all these souls! He strikes them down! Anyone who does not want to be held back by God must find the path that leads downward: the path upon which we become free of ourselves; the path upon which we must die, the path upon which we see our strength always acting wrongly and always deceiving us. Upon this path God never holds back, but he does upon every other path.

This takes place in a remarkable way. God restrains

We must find the path that leads downward.

our works by his works. It is God's works that Jesus brought to the attention of the impatient ones. But one thing offended them: the works of God made the impatient ones appear as nothing. Everything the Savior did revealed their poverty and their nothingness. When it comes, for example, to feeding thousands in the wilderness, they are just babes in arms, unable to cook their own food. When it comes to making the blind see, making the lame walk, bringing the dead back to life; when it comes to comforting the sinner and giving him aid; when it comes to forming a new people to the glory of God – then they are all nothing. Only the Lord from heaven can do this.

Look at the deceit that works inside our own souls and moves us to regard God's works as insignificant. We do this because in the sight of God we ourselves are nothing, and because at the appearance of Jesus Christ our strength is brought to shame. We persuade ourselves that something else must happen. And what is this something else? The Savior, to please us, not God, should make it possible for us to arise again and be active in the world. This is the same false path the Jews started upon as the people of God in the time of the Maccabees. They were able to reacquire crowns of laurel, and would have almost become a people of world history except that from the beginning God struck them down. Oh, you people who want to become something in the world, you people who recognize Christ Jesus and know that he is the Lord – if you want to mold yourselves according to the world and enforce your way in his name, you will be held back. The works of God will fall like a judgment, a heavy judgment, upon your heads and will crush you. You will no longer be a part of the kingdom of God.

But there are others, those who endure. They become like sheep in the presence of the works of God. In quietness a transformation takes place within them. In the works of God they immediately see their own unfitness and are glad (2 Cor. 12:7–10). They lay aside their cloaks, whether an official's cloak, a clergyman's cloak, or any other spiritual or worldly cloak. Joyfully they lay aside the crowns, which may have been placed upon their heads in the world, and exclaim, "God be praised! My works are finished. God's works begin!" They become quiet, they become humble, they become joyful and childlike. The works of God strip away every sophistication. Oh, happy are those who become like sheep following their shepherd, who can be shown more and more works of God because every work of God becomes a light for them. Every work of God shows them the part of their own nature and of their own strength, which has to be given up!

If only we Christians could understand this, the nations could be made ready for the works of God! At the moment it looks as if this will never happen. A real breakthrough among the nations has not yet come about. With all its strength the church presses forward along the wrong path. Wherever the opportunity arises to put itself forward, to play a part, to make a name for itself, to rise up in the world, there it stands ready. By the time the Savior cries out, "Stop, stop, stop! You jump around too much!" – by the time he calls after his people that they should be patient until he determines that the time is ripe, until he has prepared the nations, until he can win hearts with his deeds – the church is already far away! And the Savior is left alone.

Who is guilty? I must severely lecture the flock. The sheep are guilty. We have not learned to take care not to rush forward impatiently. Today the point is this: are you humble before God when his works are done among you? Can you let these things happen and await the kingdom joyfully and with lively freshness, even if you yourselves go without honor, even if your works must cease when confronted by God's works?

From the spiritual standpoint the most important thing is to surrender, to refrain from pushing! Surrender, I tell you. Don't push! The guilt of the sheep is that they want to push instead of to surrender. Although he loves them, the Savior is hampered when he sees his sheep entangled in the methods and means of the age. They surrender nothing and go astray. They always cry for the Savior, but when he wants to do something for them, they still will not give up their strategies. Involved in the techniques of the world, they believe this and that is how things should best be done. They continue along the accustomed paths while the Savior is left alone and the works of God make no impression. They are all so contented with how things are supposed to get done that there is not even a real hunger for God to work.

If we would just become like true sheep, then the genuine, living deeds of Jesus Christ would begin. They could begin today if we would cease to turn around ourselves with so much self-assurance. These deeds could begin right now if we would freely face God's cause and inwardly give ourselves up to it instead of always holding fast, apparently in faith, in patience, in hope, in love, but in reality holding fast only to ourselves. Thus we never quite reach what the Savior wants: Die! Give yourself! Do not be stubborn! The Savior loves you, so give him the joy of daring this. You think it will mean the end, that the Savior would also die if you were not there – but if you let yourself be led completely into death, then Jesus will live, and you will live in him (Gal. 2:20). You who do this are known to the Savior, and you will know him. He can reveal the powers of his future to you, and you will never perish. The others, having the characteristics of sheep but not doing the will of the Savior, will receive blow after blow and in the end will die. It will be

The hardest thing for us to accept about God's kingdom is that it makes us quiet.

said to them, "Away with you! I cannot use you!" And so generation after generation passes away without God's will being revealed.

Let us take this seriously, dear people. These are not small matters but matters of the utmost importance, and they show the way we must go. All our rushing around and doing and thinking this or that can certainly build us up. We can be exulted up to heaven, but these things can also become hindrances, leaving the Savior to run behind us, as it were, holding on to our coattails in order that we do not rush headlong to who-knows-where. Only when he is before us and we march behind him will he bring us through the awful pits and dangers of this present time. He can give us eternal life even among the thorns and in the midst of the abyss, uphill and downhill, wherever we stumble and fall and come to the point of death (2 Cor. 4:7–12). Oh, that our eyes might be opened! We in our "salvation" want to make death the glory of God – a happy end! – a blessed death! – but God desires to be glorified in life, here on earth. You can see by this how far we have gone astray. What we strive after is vastly different from what the Savior intended. It is simply a wrong path.

This is the collective guilt of all the sheep in this present time, even of the best ones. Therefore, we will acknowledge – for otherwise we just would not experience it – that God the Father is greater than all our human devices, religious or otherwise. Let us allow all this to sink quietly into our hearts, preserving it and bringing fruit before God in the Spirit. In tears, let us surrender ourselves to God and seek to become sheep through whom God's kingdom can be revealed in Christ. Nothing else is worthy before God.

We are workers,
not master builders –
ministers, not messiahs.
We are prophets of
a future not our own.

Oscar Romero

> **B**ecause of the oppression of the
> poor and the groaning of the needy,
> I will now arise," says the Lord.
> "I will protect them from those
> who malign them."
>
> Psalm 12:5

16

The Power of God

The Lord promises that he will arise on behalf of the poor and the needy. How? That is always a puzzle. But here we have it: "God will do it. The poor and the needy are before me and I must help them." But now, how will he do it?

A lot can be said in answer to this question. The faithless say, "Oh, yes, even in our misery he can bless us – and after all, there is eternity." But in this way not a single need is overcome, not a single tear is dried. And this business of eternity – honestly, I don't quite trust it when people console me with hopes of eternity. If I cannot see any help in this world, who can guarantee it to me in eternity? Or has the Savior come only into eternity? I say he has come to us! Therefore the comfort of eternity is not sufficient. Can we only reach the goal as soon as we leave this life behind? I don't believe so. God does not work in such a mechanical way. We cannot just merrily skip around in the world and lightly assume that when we die everything will be all right in eternity. Oh no!

Still, Christians everywhere are almost exclusively concerned with the life beyond: they believe that God is powerless on earth, and they declare it to be fanaticism if one sees the light of the living God here on earth and believes that finally even death will be abolished. People everywhere remain under the illusion that God stays eternally in heaven. People think that we are condemned to endure torture for the time we live on this small orb called earth; and after our life here we will be either condemned or blessed, depending on our religious belief. And so it goes on throughout the ages – and we are content to leave it at that.

Tear yourselves away from this unbelief! If all we aspire to is to get out of this world in order to be free in the next, then we pay tribute to sin and death. It shows the greatest disdain for all the words of God in scripture when we reject the joyous hope of God's coming reign by resigning ourselves to our fate on this earth and letting things continue as they are. Because our religious lives are bankrupt, people think that God is also bankrupt and unable to accomplish anything on earth.

Our happiness depends upon God exercising his power, not we exercising ours (Ps. 92:4). He must accomplish his will, and we must believe that he will do this. This is why God created us. And those who serve the power of God in their hearts pull a little of it down into our world. They represent God by drawing down his power to help.

It is not so much a question of a person's wanting to be converted. The first and most important thing is that God gathers him in. Our redemption consists of God's help, through deeds that we can do nothing to bring about. On that day when we have breathed our last and are before God, we shall be amazed, in looking back, at how much God had to "rise up" for us and use his power to save us, despite our will. The "rising up" of God is always a matter of his moving closer and closer to us, of fighting his way down until he can break into our world.

This is the goal of God's efforts for us. This is why help is continually delayed. Need and misery will not be overcome until the barriers between eternity and this world are broken through again. An opening must be made from above downward, not from below upward.

If I can't see any help in this world, who can guarantee it to me in the next?

We pay tribute to sin and death if all we want is to get out of this world and into eternity.

Today's Christianity sees it just the other way round. We Christians would rather find an opening out of this world. We only want to fly up and out of this world, as doves fly into the sky, and be saved. According to the Bible, however, the openings must be broken through from above in order that help can fly down to our earth. But nowadays it takes a terrible struggle to bring this about. Do you know why? Because nobody believes it! We all want to get to heaven and be saved, even though we haven't the slightest idea of what lies beyond. So many people today want things to end. Even so, when they get to "the other side," they will surely rub their eyes sore. One should think very carefully about these matters, and it is a great pain to me that Christians generally do not understand them. That is why we are in such a bad way.

I know that people will say, "There goes Blumhardt again with his cute stories." But please prove to me which of the two is biblical: our death and flight into heaven, or God's future here on earth. From the first to the last chapter, the Bible deals with the coming of God into this world, and there is nothing about this business of dying. Every word in the Bible guarantees the deeds of God right here where I stand. Down here is where Jesus appeared, not above in the invisible world, not around the throne of God. Here on earth is where he wants to dwell again. Here on earth is where we may find him. Here on earth is where he came and will come again. God only needs to lift one finger against our affliction, and more is achieved than if we founded a hundred thousand institutions. We must ask God to "rise up." We have to become biblical once again. All I wish to say is this: become biblical. Understanding and wisdom will be given if our first concern is that God comes now and that Jesus lives here. We should lay claim to our right on this earth – the right to victory over sin and death here on earth – not because of our faith, but because of God's power to make things right.

Christianity has allowed itself to be influenced by all kinds of heathen ideas: namely, to see the glory of God only in the world beyond. In this way we have lost Jesus. This adoration of Jesus in heaven will never achieve anything for us! Of course, it does give us a religious culture. But this is a sham; it obscures what should be the chief characteristic of Christians: "God in man on earth." People have no idea what Christ's coming really means. What else is this coming of Christ other than the prophetic idea that God must have a counterpart on earth? God must dwell again among humans.

Our pathetic faith accomplishes nothing. It sounds harsh, but I must say it. I can't stand it when people continually babble about heaven. They are the most self-centered people. They think only of God in relation to themselves. This is sheer folly – a fabrication of the first order. It is the power of God on this earth that redeems. Who, then, can say of his faith, "Look, I have the true faith." That is a delusion. Yet, if we turn the whole thing around and if we bear in mind God's efforts to penetrate into our world and accomplish something here on earth, then we shall truly see.

It is not sufficient to have a "religion." Unbelievers have a religion too, and it is not much different from ours. God does not care a fig about our religion. When God is unable to come down and help, he even prefers to let the people become irreligious. In Egypt, for example, the Israelites did as they liked, and they went to rack and ruin. Even so, God cared for them. His help does not depend upon our religion, but upon his faithfulness, mercy, and power, and upon hearts that wait for him to break in.

The promises are before us: "Now I will rise up. Now I will give help." We know that great help has come to us in Jesus Christ, but only if we believe that it is for this earth. Once, when Jesus had visited Cana, in Galilee, a certain royal official, whose son was dying in Capernaum, came to him and begged him to come and heal his son. Jesus told him, "Unless you people see miraculous signs and wonders, you will never believe" (John 4:48). He could have said, "Trust me – you see who I am!" Instead Jesus said, "I know that you do not trust me, so I must give you signs and wonders." There were people who trusted him without all this, of course. For them signs and wonders were an added joy, rather than a necessity. But for many, signs and wonders were essential. What would we do today if the signs and wonders of the Savior had not been written down? We would find it very difficult to preach indeed.

It is, however, both remarkable and paradoxical that those who do not long for the coming of the Savior also do not believe in signs and wonders. Miracles are only expected by those who have a longing for the coming of the Savior, for the fulfillment of time. These things are closely bound together. For those who do not have this longing, signs and wonders are a matter of complete indifference. They are even a threat! But we are willing to admit to the Savior our weakness of faith and tell him, "Yes, it is true that we need signs and wonders. Even now, during this time when we must have patience and until the time when signs and wonders will be seen everywhere, until all the wretched are truly helped – in this time of battle, we need signs and wonders."

Because our religious lives are bankrupt, we think that God is also bankrupt.

People like us believe, but why? I have, after all, experienced the power of God. I have more than enough reason to believe in miracles. I would wish this for other people too, at least enough signs and wonders in this time of darkness for sincere hearts to be refreshed. When we read about the healing works of Jesus, we cannot help but say, "Yes, dear Savior, now I must see whether or not you live." We are indeed poor souls, and nothing moves us quite like a physical jolt. And we cannot keep going very long, spiritually speaking, without a physical improvement. A break must be made through the wall of physical death if our spiritual life is to be sustained.

Thus, we should pray steadfastly for this and believe that something will happen. Something must happen here on earth. What is our chief concern? And when the Savior acts, what is his chief concern? To accomplish good on earth – physically as well as spiritually! This is actually the foundation upon which we stand. It is a sad religion, no, a worthless religion, if my body, my material and social circumstance, is racked and tormented. But our God is Lord of both heaven and earth. Therefore, we should be people who in all things have light, right through death and into resurrection. This will make us strong. He will place us in the safety for which we long.

Amen

Rejoice in the Lord always.
I will say it again: Rejoice!
Let your gentleness be evident to all.
The Lord is near…And the peace
of God, which transcends all
understanding, will guard your hearts
and your minds in Christ Jesus.

Philippians 4:4–9

17

Rejoice in the Lord

We should rejoice in the Lord. But why? We must have a reason, not just in theory but in reality. We must have something concrete in which to rejoice, not in just anything, but in Christ. It is not that all other joys should be taken away from us, but these are not the joys that last. All those things that take place on this earth, making us happy for the moment, are very short-lived. Whatever earthly joys there may be are piecemeal, and joyful moods fill our hearts only fleetingly. Alongside such moods there is also much sorrow, born of all kinds of misery.

There is much trouble, much uncertainty, and much unpeacefulness in this world. We cannot expect, therefore, to have constant joy, at least not in the way the world thinks of it. We must always be prepared for it to pass away. Yet we cannot truly live without a continuous joy, a joy that endures. We must seek this joy. We look for it in Christ because in him a new future, a new goal, has opened before us.

That is the meaning of the saying, "The Lord is near." It also expresses where the goal lies: namely, here on earth. We may rejoice in Christ because we shall still experience the good on earth with him who is the Lord of peace. We have a kingdom of the future before our eyes. This is so firmly established that we can hold fast to it and remain joyful in this hope. This is what our faith consists in, and this faith makes us firm and as hard as steel. This faith makes us defy the whole world as it is today.

This faith is not a "belief" in God, for true faith is a natural, spontaneous awareness of God. Nor is it a "belief" in Christ, for this "belief" changes into the realization: we know that Christ is. It is faith that we shall become something through God, through Christ, through the Holy Spirit. That is our faith. Our faith wants to create something; it wants to create that for which the whole of human society has been striving for thousands of years. We would have no foundation if our faith in the kingdom of God did not also believe in human happiness. Then it would rightly be said of our faith that it is false, small, weary, weak, faint-hearted, and full of doubt and fear. Then we would become unsteady and wavering people.

We know what we believe, therefore we live it.

If we dare to believe that we mortals can still represent on earth something that is right before God and humanity, if we keep our eyes on this, then we are made firm. This is not only God's will, but it is the desire of our hearts as well. This faith makes us unwavering and turns us into strong people (2 Tim. 1:6–7). Yes, it is right and true: human beings are not meant to be miserable creatures. God's offspring shall not waste away forever in sorrow and in misery. This longing lies deep in our own hearts and is so much a part of every person's heart that it cannot be uprooted.

Religious people try a different approach. They seek the future of humanity beyond the earth and want to make people happy with supernatural things. Certainly it is a strength for people in misery who are utterly at a loss to say, "One day it will all come to an end, and I will die and be at rest. Then I will be in God's hands." But this has never produced lasting strength. It has never led to a truly vigorous life. If ultimately this end to all misery is not entirely certain, then there is every reason to doubt whether we can truly rejoice in it. When I think of all the people who have come to me to talk about God and Christ and about the kingdom of heaven, I know that this thought has concerned each of them: can I not receive any help now, here, in my own life? How often have I heard people say, "Is there no God in heaven? Not in the sense that I may be blessed at some future time, but that help will be given on this earth so that I may be joyful, freed from my sins, and really become a true man or woman." This cry reaches us from millions of hearts.

If only one person wants truth and the joy of life to play the greatest part – not sorrow or distress, not misery or a sinful, perverted life – then this cry arises from millions of other hearts. Then we can proclaim, "You are right. You can believe this, and because God exists, you are right if you do not regard this present society as the ultimate one (Isa. 65:17–25). You are right too if you believe that one day there will be a church community upon earth, a society of men and women in which peace and joy will reign. You are right. Believe it! As truly as God is in heaven, as certain as Christ was born, as truly as the gospel is preached, so will there be a kingdom of God on earth! Therefore believe and hope in this kingdom, even though its fulfillment still awaits us."

Yet for those who keep their eyes on this kingdom, it is not only in the future; it is already coming into being in the present. And it *is* present, for this faith is today shaping a community of men and women, a society in which people strengthen each other towards this goal. Without such a society how is faith possible? The kingdom of God must be foreshadowed in a human society. The apostle Paul calls this society the body of Christ, of which Christ is the head (1 Cor. 12:12–27). Jesus also calls it a building, where each stone fits into the next so that the building becomes complete (1 Pet. 2:4–12). He calls it his little flock, where all love one another, where each answers for the others and all answer for the one. In the awareness that we are the fighters for the future, we are those through whom the earth must become bright. We know what we believe. Therefore we testify to what we believe; therefore, we live what we believe. In this way God's kingdom comes into the present. It comes now just as it shall be in the future.

In order to form such a society in Christ there must be people who are resolute now, people who are free now, people who are free from anxiety now. Right from the beginning, when the apostles began to preach, this freedom from anxiety was sought. But do not misunderstand this. Let me tell you, it is foolish to say to your neighbor, "Don't worry!" When a person lives utterly alone, isolated in the world, and nobody is concerned about him, when other people kick him around and want to have nothing to do with him, when a

**Only in
a shared
life can
you say,
"Don't
worry!"**

person is excluded from everything that lends human dignity to life, when there is nothing for him to do but to earn his bread with much worry, toil, and burden, then it is a sin to say to him, "Don't worry!"

Today it is coldly said of millions, "They shouldn't worry. If they would only work, they would earn their wages." Those who talk like this pass right by such folks without caring a jot for them. The majority of working people still do not have jobs worthy of a human being. They live scattered and isolated lives. What a misery it is to have to beg, or to work two jobs. Yet how many people have to do it! What an unworthy existence it is for the one who wants to meet his obligations and be a respected person but who cannot pay his taxes or his bills or is unable to serve society in any meaningful way. How can I say to such a person, "Don't worry." What coldness of heart!

No, at present the whole world lies deep in worries and cares, including the wealthiest of nations. But within the society and organism that proceeds from Christ, worries can and should cease. There we should care for one another. When the apostle Paul says, "Do not worry," he takes it for granted that these are people who are united by a bond of solidarity so that no one says anymore, "This is mine," but all say, "Our solidarity, our bond, must take away our worries. All that we share together must help each one of us and so rid us of anxiety."

In this way the kingdom of heaven comes. First it comes in a small flock free from anxiety. Thus Jesus teaches: "I tell you, do not worry about your life, what you will eat or drink; or about your body, what you will wear...But seek first God's kingdom and his righteousness, and all these things will be given to you as well" (Matt. 6:32–33). From the beginning, ever since Christ was born, people have sought such a society, a fellowship of the kingdom, free from cares and worries. There is an enormous strength when people stand together, when they unite together in a communal way. The idea of private property falls away, and they are so bound together in the Spirit that each one says, "What I have belongs to the others, and if I should ever be in need, they will help me" (2 Cor. 8:13–15). This firm and absolute standing together in a shared life where each is responsible for the other is the kind of life in which you can indeed say, "Don't worry!"

Time and again, people have attempted to live together in this way. Yet it has never come fully into being. And this is the reason why Christianity as Christ meant it has become so weak. To be sure, people throughout the ages have known that this building up of a social order in which one need not worry anymore was originally Christ's will. Christ told us not to seek after riches or the honors of this world. He said this precisely because he took it for granted that his united people would always have the necessary means for life. He told his followers that their oneness in love, their lifestyle of sharing, would provide them with sufficient food and clothing.

Again and again people have thought that this is the way society should be. But because it does not fully come about, they give it up eventually and replace it by so-called charity where those who have, out of a charitable urge, offer something to those who have not. This is the way it has always been. Many people find ways, with their extra means, to help the poor, here and there. Yet this is not what Jesus Christ wants. Just the opposite! What worries are caused by the many charitable institutions of our day. Millions continue to worry how they can get a little here and a little there. Often they are turned away by charity itself. Does this surprise you? Do not be taken aback when the philanthropists of this world fail to give help. "Charity" is not the way. It still holds back what is essentially needed. Therefore we must join together. A united company of Jesus must come about.

How shall this happen? We have lost the feeling for it. One reason why Christ's followers did not remain organically bound together, as at Pentecost, is that they wanted to draw in too many foreign elements. The members wanted to convert the whole world before they themselves were fully converted. It is simply not possible to gather hundreds of thousands of people into common fellowship before the members themselves are ready for this. This is especially so if you draw in people who are materialistic, people who are envious, people who are not free, who are not willing to go the whole way. It would be better if they remained outside and had the cares of the world. They are not fit to be co-fighters.

"Charity" is not the way. It still holds back something essential.

The freedom of the heart must first be there, a freedom from all that the world plays around with and that attracts us. Then we can shed all worries. How much people are able to do once they are freed from all cares and do not worry about their daily bread! It does not take much, only that people are so bound together that they know, "When I get into need, the others will be there." But if I say, "I will save enough for myself so that I will never have to depend on others," or if I insist on being rich and the other poor, then this is the ruin of any Christian society. It is a mockery of Christ's body.

It is for this reason I do not think much of "spiritual" communities. They do not last. People are friends for a while, but it eventually ends. Anything that is going to last must have a much deeper foundation than some kind of spiritual experience. Unless we have community in the body, in things material, we will never have it in spiritual matters (Acts 2:42–47). We are not mere spirits. We are human beings of flesh and blood. Every

If I am saved by grace, then I am a worker through grace.

day we need to eat. We need clothing for every season. We must share our tools; we must work together; we must work communally and not each for himself. Otherwise we can never become one in the love of Christ, can never become the flock, the community of Jesus, which stands up in the world and says, "Now things must become quite different. Now the individual must stop living for himself. Now a society of brothers and sisters must arise."

This is the way Jesus wants us to set aside our worries. Yet we Christians expect people to have faith in the most impossible of situations, in conditions where they nearly perish of need and misery, where they exist in wretched hovels, hardly knowing how to keep the wolf from the door. And we come along and call out to them, "Simply believe!" To shout into this kind of distress, "Believe! Then everything will be all right, heaven awaits you!" is an unreasonable demand that cannot be carried out (James 2:14–18). No, the kingdom of God must not be only a kingdom of the future. Certainly for the vast majority it still lies in the future, but in Christ's church community we should seek to become united, and begin to become free in such a way that, at least in the circles where we love one another, cares cease.

Our community must be stronger than the gates of death and hell. It must be of sterling quality in every aspect, not only communal but also truthful. No one who happens to have this or that advantage should even think he should be especially honored. It is a matter of God's virtues, not human ones. Not customs, not people's views, not the latest trend, not what a nation happens to believe is right, but only what is right before God. When this happens, God's people will be hated. For it tells the whole world straight to its face, "Your customs are false! Do you suppose we recognize your warlike ways? Do you think we are impressed by your pride and envy, your self-love, your whole swindle of being rich? No! We would rather belong to the destitute than go on doing homage to this swindle!" The community of Jesus Christ draws hatred upon itself because it asserts itself in this way. It no longer wants the ways of the world, the latest ideas – what we want is God and his Lordship!

This causes a violent struggle, which is why the Savior says, "The gate is narrow and the way is hard that leads to life, and only a few find it" (Matt. 7:14). Most people, including Christians, admire this world. They pay homage to it. When the prince of this world comes and offers his riches to them, they do not do what the Savior did. He said, "Be gone! I will not rule by your means." Most people, when Satan comes, bow down before him and say, "Oh, yes, I am sure I can reconcile my relationship to God with the acceptance of worldly honor, praise, and wealth from you. And actually things will go much better afterwards!" This is what most of us do, and therefore we now see many Christians who are completely of the world.

Do not deceive yourselves! It is not only the unbelievers. In fact, I know unbelievers who demonstrate more faith than the believers. The believers are the very ones who are in danger of seeking honor and of shining before men in their piety, and saying, "Yes! Yes!" to everything. On top of it all, they appeal to the Bible. It is no good just to throw bible texts around. For there are those who do not use a single bible quotation anymore, and yet they fight for God, for truth, for love, for fellowship. They fight for the betterment of the poor so that they may at last come out of their misery. They may not use the name of God, but I believe they shall hear the words, "Go into the joy of your Lord." – "I do not know what I have done to serve You." – "Yes, yes! You served me. Whatever you did to relieve human misery, whatever you tried to do to make things better on earth, that you did to me." Who knows but that these same unbelievers will not be the majority of those who enter the kingdom of heaven, for it is sterling quality that matters here.

People of faith must achieve something tangible. Never think you do not have to achieve something. It has been preached to us that we are only saved through grace. I believe that. But if I have been saved by grace, then I must achieve something. You may, as a favor, be accepted as a partner in a business; but once in it, you are told to get to work. Neither in heaven nor on earth is it possible just to settle down comfortably in something called grace and do nothing and care for nobody else. If I am saved by grace, then I am a worker through grace (Eph. 2:8–10). If I am justified by grace, then through grace I am a worker for justice. If through grace I am placed within the truth, then through grace I am a servant of truth. If through grace I have been placed within peace, then through grace I am a servant of peace. To take away for myself something given through grace and to care nothing about others – that is not the right way. Whatever I am through grace makes me a worker, and only the worker counts; the slacker, never.

If you want unending joy, sacrifice yourself.

In God's eyes only the worker is something. Therefore we should always consider in our hearts: what is God's will? But oh, this we cannot do! How can one possibly do that? This is where the denial of self begins. It is God's will. Therefore it is my will too, and it becomes my heart's very own property. I want it because God wants it, and it must come about because it is the will of God. For this I will stand, and for it I will give my body and my life. This is the way that we can truly offer our lives, be living sacrifices for God, and truly work through this sacrifice, this sacrifice of our whole lives.

There is great strength in this, my dear friends. Sacrifice yourself, for once, for the will of God! It will not be in vain. Sacrifice yourself for the truth, for God's justice. Sacrifice yourself, against human reason, for something that is truly good. Sacrifice yourself for Christ in all things, for the church community that seeks the kingdom of God. There is tremendous strength in this. In times past, thousands have been driven to their death because of this. They gave their lives joyfully, even when most cruelly tortured. They remained strong because they stood firm in the will of God. Nowadays people shun every cross. Nobody dares anything anymore. No one risks anything. We cower as soon as something runs contrary to the way things are. We fear what others think. But if we want to have joy in Christ, unending joy, then we must learn to sacrifice ourselves. There is no other way. Things will never be better in the world unless self-sacrificing people offer themselves as workers for God. A comfortable Christianity will never change the world.

No, rejoice in the Lord, in the hope of his kingdom! Rejoice in the Lord as resolute fighters of his church community, the community in which brothers and sisters are able to live with one another in true self-denial and freedom, the church community that does not condemn but has clear eyes for the truth. Be bound together in this! Stand up for God's future, and your joy will be lasting. Whoever is gripped by this Christ will win the fight. He will always have before his eyes the day when all people will be able to rejoice after the battle is won for the glory of God.

Afterword
by Karl Barth

I must post a warning for those from theological circles, as well as for those who think only politically. You might have the misfortune to lay aside this book, discontented and disappointed after browsing through it a few times. We cannot read it as we are prone to read other books and articles. Blumhardt puts forward no guiding principles. He produces no historical and psychological conclusions. He speaks neither politics nor theology. There is no speculative probing into problems, or drawing conclusions, or building systems. He refutes nobody, and nobody needs to feel refuted by him, but he does not concur with anybody else's views either. He pins down neither himself nor anyone else with precise principles.

In fact, Blumhardt does not expound a particular point of view. Rather, he lets us experience the echo that the Bible aroused within him every day. He does not want to say anything brilliant, set off any fireworks, or strike any blow: he simply tells us the divine truth in the world as it meets him. I suspect that he would have quite a few things to say about the conflicts and prob-

From *Der Freie Schweitzer Arbeiter*, September 1916, in response to Blumhardt's *Morgen-Andachten*.

lems that stir us nowadays. He will not say it, though; it is not important enough to him because other things are more important. He evidently expects the answer on a different level.

Shall we take exception to the fact that Blumhardt sidesteps a whole host of problems? No. We already have much literature on certain questions regarding the consummation of God's future, but hardly a single book like this one that we can share with unmitigated joy with all sorts of people who also want to hope with us. One of the deepest impressions I get from Blumhardt is that here we meet a priestly person. Blumhardt can do something which most of us cannot do: represent God's cause in the world yet not wage war on the world, love the world and yet be completely faithful to God, suffer with the world and speak a frank word about its need while simultaneously going beyond this to speak the redemptive word about the help it awaits. He is able to carry the world up to God and bring God down into the world, pleading unceasingly and unwaveringly before God and to God, "Your kingdom come!" and waiting and hastening with others toward this coming. Is that not the highest and most promising thing a person can do – if he or she can?

Another strong impression I get throughout – at bottom identical with the first – is how organic truth is in the eyes of this man. He does not construe, neither does he hack to pieces. He does not demonstrate or engage in polemics. Not for a moment does the misery of the human condition become an independent object of his interest; it lies embedded from the very beginning in the coming of God. He sees God creating light out of darkness, one taking shape out of the other and growing under his rulership. Blumhardt's vision is an unparalleled, joyful triumph over those who are given to speculative dissection.

Blumhardt always begins with God's presence, power, and purpose. He starts out from God. He does not begin by climbing upwards to him by means of contemplation and deliberation. God is the end, and because we already know him as the beginning, we may await his consummating acts. Blumhardt has faith in God's revelation because he already sees it in the nearest and most ordinary things. He believes in the victory of God because he sees evil also as never quite outside God's circle. Out of this primary recognition Blumhardt confronts two realities: on the one hand he has insight into the need of the world, and on the other hand he possesses the joyful hope of its being overcome. No one and no condition is outside God's great circle. Alongside our weak nature is God's power. In this way, from the very beginning, human nature too is requisitioned for God, and that in a very far-reaching way.

The deep suffering that Blumhardt feels for the actual situation of the world and his confident expectations for its future are grounded from the outset in a joyful trust in God's creation, which is, after all, simple trust in God. He never loses sight of the great interconnections through which evil too must become subject to the will of God. Blumhardt's faith in God's providence is the natural outcome of his hope in a new heaven and a new earth, and that truth shall enter into people's hearts. Hence, even war has a meaning. Blumhardt looks upon such eventualities as a judgment, except that for him this term has no gloomy and tragic meaning, but chiefly a joyful and hopeful one. "We could say that it is times of judgment alternating with times of grace that help us forward toward salvation." For – and here lies the key to everything – with Jesus the good, the powers of the future, have actually already begun, the good to which the world and nature alike are called, which towers right into our own time also and goes forward toward a consummation.

But how shall all this become reality? Blumhardt has two answers: the one he gives to God, "Only you, O God, can help, none other!" The other he gives to us, "Ask. Ask and you shall receive. And in asking we share in, we help with, the new creation." Blumhardt sees the coming kingdom being prepared in a double movement in heaven and on earth, and the actual decision lies not in the visible but in the invisible world. If something new is to arise on earth, God ultimately has to do it, but for our part we can sow truth and justice. In quite a natural way, therefore, Blumhardt comes to a concept that is very important to him – the biblical concept of the little flock, God's Zion, who gather around Christ not for their own salvation but for the redemption of the world. They are to represent God's cause, God's future, in a special way. Gathering and waiting fit hand in glove.

What will such people have to do? One thing above all: to know and to become deep and firm in the knowledge that "our actual doing must come from the strength of God." Such people are best described by what they do not do. This attitude – quiet, eagerly expectant, and directed toward God – is what Blumhardt calls "waiting." It would be good not to pass lightly over the profound depth of what he means by this, because all too often a comfortable sort of nonsense is made out of this concept. Blumhardt's meaning is that waiting, although turned inward at first, is in its essence revolutionary: "Lord God, make new! Make us new!" To act – to "wait" – means just the opposite of sitting comfortably and going along with the way things are, with the old order of things. For Blumhardt, divine and human action are closely interlocked, not in a mechanical but in an organic sense. It is our calling, our task in everyday life, that people can see the Savior through us.

When we "hasten and wait" toward God like this, the consummation is prepared, coming from God himself. Out of what is now present, and in those who live expectantly in the power of God, the future is built up quietly and inconspicuously. When will it finally appear? What is needed for this to happen in an outer way? Such questions are irrelevant. For those who await God's coming, behind everything lies the great future of God.